W9-AWX-931

Victims and
Victims' Rights

CRIME, JUSTICE, AND PUNISHMENT

Victims and Victims' Rights

Sara Faherty

Austin Sarat, GENERAL EDITOR

CHELSEA HOUSE PUBLISHERS
Philadelphia

Frontis: *Memorial to Polly Klaas, a 12-year-old murder victim.*

Chelsea House Publishers

Editor in Chief Stephen Reginald
Managing Editor James D. Gallagher
Production Manager Pamela Loos
Art Director Sara Davis
Director of Photography Judy L. Hasday
Senior Production Editor Lisa Chippendale

Staff for VICTIMS AND VICTIMS' RIGHTS

Senior Editor John Ziff
Associate Art Director/Designer Takeshi Takahashi
Picture Researcher Gillian Speeth
Cover Illustration Janet Hamlin

First Printing

1 3 5 7 9 8 6 4 2

The Chelsea House World Wide Web site address is
http://www.chelseahouse.com

Library of Congress Cataloging-in-Publication Data

Faherty, Sara.
Victims and victims' rights / Sara Faherty.
    p. cm. — (Crime, justice, and punishment)
Includes bibliographical references and index.
Summary: Explores victims and victims' rights from various perspectives, including the psychological consequences of victimization, the divergent responses of victims seeking justice and emotional healing, and the tension between granting the wishes of victims and protecting the rights of criminal defendants.

ISBN 0-7910-4308-8

1. Victims of crimes—Government policy—United States—Juvenile literature. 2. Victims of crimes—Civil rights—United States—Juvenile literature. 3. Victims of crimes—Legal status, laws, etc.—United States—Juvenile literature. [1. Victims of crimes.] I. Title. II. Series.
HV6250.3.U5F53   1999
362.88'0973—dc21
                                           98-36531
                                              CIP
                                              AC

Contents

CRIME, JUSTICE, AND PUNISHMENT

Fears and Fascinations:

An Introduction to Crime, Justice, and Punishment

By Austin Sarat

We live with crime and images of crime all around us. Crime evokes in most of us a deep aversion, a feeling of profound vulnerability, but it also evokes an equally deep fascination. Today, in major American cities the fear of crime is a major fact of life, some would say a disproportionate response to the realities of crime. Yet the fear of crime is real, palpable in the quickened steps and furtive glances of people walking down darkened streets. At the same time, we eagerly follow crime stories on television and in movies. We watch with a "who done it" curiosity, eager to see the illicit deed done, the investigation undertaken, the miscreant brought to justice and given his just deserts. On the streets the presence of crime is a reminder of our own vulnerability and the precariousness of our taken-for-granted rights and freedoms. On television and in the movies the crime story gives us a chance to probe our own darker motives, to ask "Is there a criminal within?" as well as to feel the collective satisfaction of seeing justice done.

Fear and fascination, these two poles of our engagement with crime, are, of course, only part of the story. Crime is, after all, a major social and legal problem, not just an issue of our individual psychology. Politicians today use our fear of, and fascination with, crime for political advantage. How we respond to crime, as well as to the political uses of the crime issue, tells us a lot about who we are as a people as well as what we value and what we tolerate. Is our response compassionate or severe? Do we seek to understand or to punish, to enact an angry vengeance or to rehabilitate and welcome the criminal back into our midst? The CRIME, JUSTICE, AND PUNISHMENT series is designed to explore these themes, to ask why we are fearful and fascinated, to probe the meanings and motivations of crimes and criminals and of our responses to them, and, finally, to ask what we can learn about ourselves and the society in which we live by examining our responses to crime.

Crime is always a challenge to the prevailing normative order and a test of the values and commitments of law-abiding people. It is sometimes a Raskolnikov-like act of defiance, an assertion of the unwillingness of some to live according to the rules of conduct laid out by organized society. In this sense, crime marks the limits of the law and reminds us of law's all-too-regular failures. Yet sometimes there is more desperation than defiance in criminal acts; sometimes they signal a deep pathology or need in the criminal. To confront crime is thus also to come face-to-face with the reality of social difference, of class privilege and extreme deprivation, of race and racism, of children neglected, abandoned, or abused whose response is to enact on others what they have experienced themselves. And occasionally crime, or what is labeled a criminal act, represents a call for justice, an appeal to a higher moral order against the inadequacies of existing law.

Figuring out the meaning of crime and the motivations of criminals and whether crime arises from defiance, desperation, or the appeal for justice is never an easy task. The motivations and meanings of crime are as varied as are the persons who engage in criminal conduct. They are as mysterious as any of the mysteries of the human soul. Yet the desire to know the secrets of crime and the criminal is a strong one, for in that knowledge may lie one step on the road to protection, if not an assurance of one's own personal safety. Nonetheless, as strong as that desire may be, there is no available technology that can allow us to know the whys of crime with much confidence, let alone a scientific certainty. We can, however, capture something about crime by studying the defiance, desperation, and quest for justice that may be associated with it. Books in the Crime, Justice, and Punishment series will take up that challenge. They tell stories of crime and criminals, some famous, most not, some glamorous and exciting, most mundane and commonplace.

This series will, in addition, take a sober look at American criminal justice, at the procedures through which we investigate crimes and identify criminals, at the institutions in which innocence or guilt is determined. In these procedures and institutions we confront the thrill of the chase as well as the challenge of protecting the rights of those who defy our laws. It is through the efficiency and dedication of law enforcement that we might capture the criminal; it is in the rare instances of their corruption or brutality that we feel perhaps our deepest betrayal. Police, prosecutors, defense lawyers, judges, and jurors administer criminal justice and in their daily actions give substance to the guarantees of the Bill of Rights. What is an adversarial system of justice? How does it work? Why do we have it? Books in the Crime, Justice, and Punishment series will examine the thrill of the chase as we seek to capture the criminal. They will also reveal the drama and majesty of the criminal trial as well as the day-to-day reality of a criminal justice system in which trials are the exception and negotiated pleas of guilty are the rule.

When the trial is over or the plea has been entered, when we have separated the innocent from the guilty, the moment of punishment has arrived. The injunction to punish the guilty, to respond to pain inflicted by inflicting pain, is as old as civilization itself. "An eye for an eye and a tooth for a tooth" is a biblical reminder that punishment must measure pain for pain. But our response to the criminal must be better than and different from the crime itself. The biblical admonition, along with the constitutional prohibition of "cruel and unusual punishment," signals that we seek to punish justly and to be just not only in the determination of who can and should be punished, but in how we punish as well. But neither reminder tells us what to do with the wrongdoer. Do we rape the rapist, or burn the home of the arsonist? Surely justice and decency say no. But, if not, then how can and should we punish? In a world in which punishment is neither identical to the crime nor an automatic response to it, choices must be made and we must make them. Books in the CRIME, JUSTICE, AND PUNISHMENT series will examine those choices and the practices, and politics, of punishment. How do we punish and why do we punish as we do? What can we learn about the rationality and appropriateness of today's responses to crime by examining our past and its responses? What works? Is there, and can there be, a just measure of pain?

CRIME, JUSTICE, AND PUNISHMENT brings together books on some of the great themes of human social life. The books in this series capture our fear and fascination with crime and examine our responses to it. They remind us of the deadly seriousness of these subjects. They bring together themes in law, literature, and popular culture to challenge us to think again, to think anew, about subjects that go to the heart of who we are and how we can and will live together.

*   *   *   *   *

Recently, legal systems in the United States and Europe have been confronted by stern challenges in the name of victims' rights. Here and abroad a tide of resentment is rising against a system of public justice that allegedly appropriates and then silences the voice of the victim. The tendency of criminal justice systems in Western democracies is to displace the victim, to shut the door on those with the greatest interest in seeing justice done. In response, victims are demanding that their voices be heard throughout the criminal justice process. And in place after place their demands have been met.

Yet the idea that victims need rights or that the victim has been superseded in modern law is somewhat odd. Victims are always present. Almost every criminal trial centers on an extended verbal reconstruction of the victim's injury. The suffering of the victim measures, in substantial part, the guilt of the offender. Nowhere was this more apparent than in prosecutor Marcia Clark's closing argument in the murder trial of O. J. Simpson.

"Usually," Clark said in one of the most watched events in the history of the American legal system,

> I feel like I'm the only one left to speak for the victims. But in this case, Ron and Nicole, they're speaking to you. They're speaking to you. And they're telling you who murdered them. . . . And they both are telling you who did it with their hair, their clothes, their bodies, their blood. They tell you he did it. He did it. Mr. Simpson, Orenthal James Simpson, he did it. They told you in the only way they can. Will you hear them? Or will you ignore their plea for justice? Or as Nicole said to Detective Edwards, "You never do anything about him." Will you?

This prosecutor, and most others, spoke not only for "the People" but also as the "only one left to speak for the victims."

Nonetheless, the victims' rights movement wants more. It seeks participation and power by making the victim the symbolic heart of modern legality. The victims' rights movement contests the dominance of legal and procedural constraints that make the justice system distant and unresponsive to crime victims' grief and rage. By transforming courts into sites for the rituals of grieving, that movement seeks to make private experiences part of public discourse. Yet in so doing not only is a private colonization of public processes encouraged, but public scrutiny invades some of the most personal aspects of our lives—the ways we suffer and grieve. It scrambles categories by allowing victims to use legal processes to express their intimate grief and private rage as they, or their surrogates, seek to enlist the loyalty of judges and juries in a quest for revenge.

Victims and Victims' Rights provides a gripping account of the pain and suffering that lie behind every criminal trial. It examines the way victims are treated in the criminal justice system and documents their struggle for greater recognition. Drawing on examples from famous cases—the Oklahoma City bombing and Karla Faye Tucker—this book acquaints us with the psychology of the victim and traces steps victims take to bring order back into their lives. It carefully describes the way the Supreme Court has dealt with the claims of victims, first rejecting and then endorsing their desire to make statements in the sentencing of those who have injured them. Throughout, it asks how victims of crime find closure and a renewed sense of security in the traumatic aftermath of crime. *Victims and Victims' Rights* is a profoundly important and morally serious inquiry into the human consequences of crime.

Victims and Victims' Rights

Jannie Coverdale holds photos of her grandsons Aaron and Elijah,
who were among the 168 people killed in the bombing of the Alfred
P. Murrah Federal Building in Oklahoma City. Behind Coverdale is
the site where the building once stood.

Jannie Coverdale was 57 when she lost her two young grandsons, Aaron and Elijah. The boys had been at American Kids, a second-floor day care center inside the Alfred P. Murrah Federal Building on the morning of April 19, 1995, when a massive truck bomb exploded in the parking lot. The blast destroyed the Murrah building, killing 168 people, 19 of them babies and young children.

Two men, Timothy J. McVeigh and Terry L. Nichols, were ultimately arrested and charged with planning and carrying out the bombing. McVeigh was found guilty of murder and sentenced to death by a federal jury. In a separate federal trial, Nichols was convicted of the lesser charge of involuntary manslaughter, and, because the jury could not agree on imposing the death penalty, he was spared the possibility of execution.

The outcome of the Nichols trial infuriated some of the victims' family members. Jannie Coverdale angrily told a *New York Times* reporter that she had a message for the jury, "and the message is that the next time someone drives a truck up to a building with a bomb and blows that building up, I hope that their loved ones are not in the building."

Given the immensity of her loss, Coverdale's emotion is understandable. Yet the private anger or pain of a victim has always played a limited role in the American criminal justice system. Ours is a public system of justice, a system in which the state assumes responsibility for dealing with the criminal and which defines the "victim" of a crime not so much as the individual harmed but as the public order. (It's not accidental that the prosecution is identified as "the People.")

Earlier societies treated crimes as private problems between the offender and the victim. For example, if someone stole something, the person who owned it was expected, at minimum, to steal it back. If someone physically harmed another person, the victim—often with the help of family members—was obliged to inflict harm upon the offender in return. The family of a murder victim paid back the killer by murdering him or members of his family. This act, in turn, called for revenge against the family of the original victim. In this way one criminal act begat another and blood feuds—bitter cycles of revenge between families—were born.

Over time, people began to recognize private justice as a threat to the stability of society, and rulers started placing limits on revenge in order to keep the peace. As kings and lords became more powerful, they attempted to construct legal systems that would put the authority to punish wrongdoers in their hands. This process was gradual, occurring over the course of many centuries, and for a long time there existed a mixture of both private justice and the king's laws. Always, however, the trend was away from personal revenge and toward public law.

As this trend continued, the role of the victim steadily diminished. While once the victim played the role of police, judge, jury, and executioner, in the modern criminal justice system he or she is simply a witness, someone who happened to be present when the offender broke a law. The investigation, prosecution, and punishment of crime are all carried out by state actors on behalf of the state—not the victim—because crime is seen first and foremost as a violation of the state's laws, not as a private matter between the offend-er and the victim. This becomes obvious in the light of *attempted* criminal acts.

Suppose, for example, that because of a mechanical failure the Oklahoma City truck bomb had not deto-nated. In that case there would have been no actual vic-tims. Yet McVeigh and Nichols would still have been punished for their attempt to do harm, because their actions demonstrated a willingness to break the law.

Where there are actual victims of a crime, these victims, like Jannie Coverdale, sometimes express exas-peration or anger at their treatment by the criminal justice system. That system, they believe, marginalizes them and ignores their needs—often in the name of protecting the rights of offenders and accused offenders. In response to this dissatisfaction, a movement to secure victims' rights has arisen.

This book explores victims and victims' rights from various perspectives, including the psychological con-sequences of victimization, the divergent responses of victims seeking justice and emotional healing, and, most important, the tension between granting the wishes of victims and protecting the rights of criminal defendants. In short, it attempts to shed light on the question of what is the proper role of victims in crimi-nal justice.

THE
TREATMENT
OF VICTIMS

R oberta Roper's contact with the criminal justice system began after a tragic and traumatic event: the brutal rape and murder of her 21-year-old daughter Stephanie. The pain of losing a child to violent crime was compounded by the way Roper was treated by the state of Maryland. Although she was informed about various proceedings, no one bothered to notify her when those proceedings were "continued," or postponed. As a result, Roper would drive for an hour and 15 minutes only to discover that a pretrial hearing had been canceled. At the trial, when she took the stand to testify, she was asked only to identify Stephanie's belongings and a photograph of the car her daughter was driving the night she was killed.

Friends of a murder victim comfort one another. In recent years frustration with the criminal justice system has led victims and their loved ones to demand a greater role in the government's response to crime.

What made Roper most furious, however, was the fact that she and her husband were excluded from the courtroom during most of the trial. This was because the defense attorneys asked the judge to enforce Maryland's "rule on witnesses"—a rule that prohibits witnesses from listening to the testimony of any other witness, in theory because it might influence what they say. Roper thinks defense attorneys invoked the rule for a different reason, though. "They didn't want [Stephanie] to seem real," she maintains, "just a name on a piece of paper. We felt disenfranchised, like what we were going through didn't matter. I literally stood outside the courtroom doors with my nose pressed against the glass."

Crime victims, including the loved ones of people who have been murdered, frequently characterize their experiences with the understaffed and undersensitive justice system as a secondary victimization. Police officers who deal with violence and death all the time may be oblivious to the fact that for victims a serious crime is a rare and terrifying ordeal. Prosecutors want victims to participate when their testimony is needed, but they may feel that the presence of victims is unnecessary—

Victims' Search for Meaning

Dean Kilpatrick, a psychologist and director of the Crime Victims Research and Treatment Center at the Medical University of South Carolina, explains how painful it is when a family thinks a loved one's death was a total waste. "The worst part is murder is a senseless, tragic, meaningless act, out of which no obvious good can come. And that's a hard thing to deal with if it's your spouse or your kid or whatever who was killed. . . . You'll see people spend a great deal of time trying to glean some degree of meaning out of what happened. And if they can't find it, they'll try to create some meaning, to show that this did not happen for no reason—that something good was meant to come out of all this."

Dr. Kilpatrick explains that the way a family is treated by the criminal justice system affects this process. If they are treated with respect, kept informed, and allowed to have input in the case, they feel society valued their loved one. If they are mistreated by the court system, that mistreatment can make the pain of their loss even worse.

or worse, gets in the way—at other points in a criminal proceeding, such as during pretrial hearings. And the court system at times seems to have little consideration for victims, requiring them to rearrange their lives and schedules so that they can appear whenever the court demands yet paying scant attention to their physical and emotional needs.

Over the last two decades, in response to their deep frustrations with the criminal justice system, crime victims have formed advocacy groups and called for changes in the way victims are treated. In her article "The Wrongs of Victims' Rights," University of Indiana–Bloomington law professor Lynne Henderson traces the development of the victims' rights movement, which, she believes, was partly the result of a backlash against defendants' rights.

Realizing that the criminal justice system could become a David versus Goliath struggle—an unequal contest between the relatively powerless individual accused and the extremely powerful state—the framers of the United States Constitution gave suspects a number of important rights, including the right to due process of the law, the right to counsel, the right not to be unreasonably searched, the right to confront witnesses in court, and the right to avoid self-incrimination. Over the years, the courts extended protections of the rights afforded the accused, narrowing the circumstances under which police could claim to have probable cause for a search, guaranteeing suspects the right to an attorney upon arrest, and compelling police to inform suspects of their right to remain silent and to have an attorney present during questioning. All of these developments contributed to a feeling that defendants were "given all the rights" and that the criminal justice system treated people who had done bad things better than it treated their innocent victims. The justice system could only respond that it did not "treat" victims at all. Rather, victims were just witnesses, and they did not need the "rights" granted to defendants because the state was not trying to take away their liberty or their life. The state's argument may have been logically sound, but it left victims dissatisfied. Maybe justice professionals didn't think the criminal trial should be mostly about the victim, but the victim and his or her family usually did.

At the same time, Americans began to react against the liberal view of the causes of crime, a view that sociologists and criminologists made prominent beginning at midcentury and that blamed such societal factors as poverty, alienation, lack of educational opportunities, and racial and ethnic discrimination. Henderson considers several possible explanations for why this view of crime lost favor: perhaps it was because of a real or perceived increase in the crime rate; perhaps because issues of crime became linked with racial issues, and liberals could not address that link; or perhaps because of an increase in gruesome crimes and the accompanying increase in media attention to crime.

Politics—particularly the renaissance of conservatism—played a role also. Conservatives promised to "get tough" on crime, complaining that liberals were too sympathetic toward criminals. Conservatives insisted that crime is simply a result of individual choice—that criminals do bad things because they are bad people. The best way to stop people from choosing to commit crimes, conservatives maintained, was to ensure swift and certain punishment, yet all the rights defendants had been granted made it impossible for the police and courts to do this job.

Henderson speculates that conservatives were glad to reintroduce the notion of the individual victim into the justice system. The liberal's David versus Goliath portrayal of an individual defendant in an uneven fight against the powerful state was hard to answer and hard to ignore. By putting the individual victim at the center of the system, conservatives could make it look

Around midcentury, sociologists and criminologists began to popularize the view that societal factors such as poverty, alienation, lack of educational opportunities, and discrimination caused crime. That view, which implicitly regarded criminals sympathetically, gradually gave way to a get-tough attitude toward crime and a greater focus on the plight of victims.

as though it was a more even fight again—one bad offender against one innocent victim.

Victims and their advocates have asked for various changes in the way the justice system treats them. In general, their requests fall into three categories: being treated with respect and sensitivity, including having their needs considered; being informed of criminal proceedings and being permitted to attend those proceedings; and being heard at various points in the process.

Among the specific requests in the first category are minor conveniences such as comfortable courthouse waiting rooms, on-site day care, transportation services, and fewer time delays, along with more significant needs such as protection from intimidation by the offender (a need especially felt by victims of organized crime or gangs). Technically, none of the requests in this category qualify as victims' rights; they are merely courtesies. Not surprisingly, these requests are not at all controversial, for while they cost some money, they require only minor changes in the way the criminal justice system operates and have no impact on anybody else's rights. And just about everyone would agree that victims deserve to be treated with special consideration.

The second category of victim requests—being informed and being present—embraces actual victims' rights, and it is somewhat more controversial than extending common courtesies to victims. Like Roberta Roper, countless victims have chafed at not being informed when judicial proceedings are scheduled (or rescheduled) and at being deliberately excluded from a hearing. Advocates say victims should have the right to attend any and all public proceedings relevant to their case, and they should have the right to timely notification of when these proceedings will take place. Although such rights have little if any effect on the rights of criminal suspects, they do impose somewhat of a burden on the courts. A criminal case can involve many hearings before the actual trial. Some of these proceedings, including arraignment and evidentiary hearings, are fairly routine and may last only a few minutes. If victims must be notified several days in advance in order to give them the opportunity to attend, there is the potential to further slow down already overburdened courts.

The third category of victims' requests—being heard—is by far the most controversial, and it is

arguably the most important. The desire to be heard is a reaction against the diminished role of victims in the modern criminal justice system: victims want the emotional satisfaction of actively participating in the government's response to crimes. Being heard can mean several things. It can mean delivering to the court a "victim impact statement," which allows victims to talk about the effect the crime has had on them (usually during the penalty phase of a trial or at a sentencing hearing). Victim impact statements are usually more gratifying than the narrow factual testimony victims are typically called on to give (such as the timing of the crime or the defendant's physical characteristics) because such statements bring the life of the victim into focus. Being heard can also mean endorsing or rejecting a plea agreement before it is

The right to speak to the court at various stages in a criminal proceeding is among victims' most important and controversial demands.

offered to a defendant or speaking at a convicted offender's parole hearing. Allowing victims to be heard may adversely affect the rights of accused offenders and convicts, and that is what makes this category of victims' rights controversial.

Since the early 1980s, victims' rights groups have won a string of victories. In 1982 California became the first state to amend its constitution to include a "victims' bill of rights," and as of 1998 a total of 28 states had followed suit, changing their constitutions to guarantee certain rights to crime victims. Some of the rights granted are quite specific—for example, the right to be notified of various hearings and to comment at those hearings, the right to access to the prosecution, the right to timely notification of an offender's release or escape, and the right to collect restitution (money to make up for the harm done) from the offender. Other state constitutional amendments are more vague. For example, Rhode Island amended its constitution to guarantee its citizens the right to be treated with "dignity and respect" by the criminal justice system. In addition to the 29 states that have constitutionally guaranteed victims' rights, all the states have enacted statutes covering the treatment of victims in the justice system.

The federal government also has moved to address the concerns of victims. In 1982 Congress passed the Victim and Witness Protection Act. Two years later, it passed the Victims of Crime Act of 1984, which established the Office of Victims of Crime to oversee funds earmarked for victim services. Later crime bills included a "victims' bill of rights" and established mandatory restitution for victims.

Despite the gains made at the state and federal levels, however, some victims' rights groups believe that an amendment to the U.S. Constitution is needed to guarantee all victims the rights they deserve. The Constitution, these groups point out, guarantees 15

specific rights to people accused of crimes. It is fundamentally unfair, they say, that victims have no constitutional protections.

An organization called the National Victims
Constitutional Amendment proposed the following
amendment, which would require every state to extend
at least 11 rights to crime victims:

> To ensure that the victim is treated with fairness, dignity,
> and respect, from the occurrence of a crime of violence
> and other crimes . . . and throughout the criminal,
> military, and juvenile justice process, as a matter of fun-
> damental rights to liberty, justice and due process, the
> victim shall have the following rights: to be informed of
> and given the opportunity to be present at every pro-
> ceeding in which those rights are extended to the accused

*President Clinton, who
supports a victims' rights
constitutional amendment,
signs a bill requiring that
communities be notified of
the release of sex offenders
and that these offenders register with local police. At
left are the parents and sib-
lings of Megan Kanka,
whose abduction and mur-
der by a repeat sex offender
led to the bill.*

or convicted offender; to be heard at any proceeding involving sentencing, including the right to object to a previously negotiated plea, or a release from custody; to be informed of any release or escape; and to a speedy trial, a final conclusion free from unreasonable delay, full restitution from the convicted offender, reasonable measures to protect the victim from violence or intimidation by the accused or convicted offender, and notice of the victim's rights.

In 1996 Senators Dianne Feinstein of California and Jon Kyl of Arizona introduced a victims' rights constitutional amendment closely resembling the one proposed by the National Victims Constitutional Amendment. However, defense lawyers, district attorneys, constitutional scholars, and many of Feinstein and Kyl's congressional colleagues immediately objected to some of the proposed amendment's provisions. They worried, for example, that an inadvertent failure to notify a victim of all the hearings pertaining to his or her case might expose the government or public employees to a lawsuit for violation of the victim's constitutional rights. They were concerned that the victim's right to a speedy trial might adversely affect prosecutors' workloads and trial preparations. They wondered whether indigent victims would be entitled to a court-provided attorney to help them exercise their rights, just as indigent defendants are entitled to a court-appointed attorney to defend them. But they believed that the potential problems associated with these rights paled in comparison with the consequences of giving victims the right to object to a previously negotiated plea arrangement.

Many victims, especially those who have suffered emotionally from a crime of violence, are appalled to learn that their attacker has pleaded guilty to a lesser crime before the trial and has received a more lenient sentence than he or she would have if convicted on the original charges. The victim's dismay, while understandable, may not evidence a clear understanding of the court system. Largely because prosecutors don't have the resources to try every case in court, the vast majority of criminal cases are settled before trial through a process known as plea bargaining. In plea bargaining, the prosecutor offers the defendant a "discount"—a lesser charge—in exchange for not making the state conduct a trial. This not only saves taxpayers money but also avoids the possibility that the defendant will be acquitted by a jury and receive no punishment at all. In determining the appropriate plea to offer, the prosecutor is supposed to estimate the merits of the case, the strength of the evidence, and the probable cost of conducting a trial. Unfortunately, these are factors the victim is not in a position to know about. Giving victims the power to approve or disapprove of pleas could throw district attorneys' offices into chaos. It could also lead to arbitrary results, since one victim might trust the prosecutor's estimation of the appropriate offer, while another might insist that a less culpable offender be prosecuted more rigorously.

In an attempt to address the concerns of critics, Feinstein and Kyl produced dozens of revised drafts of the victims' rights amendment, toning down many of the more controversial elements of the original. The new amendment they introduced in April 1998 read as follows:

SECTION 1. Each victim of a crime of violence shall have the rights to reasonable notice of, and not to be excluded from, all public proceedings relating to the crime—

to be heard, if present, and to submit a statement at all public proceedings to determine a release from custody, an acceptance of a negotiated plea, or a sentence;

to the foregoing rights at a parole proceeding that is not public, to the extent those rights are afforded to the convicted offender;

to reasonable notice of a release or escape from custody relating to the crime;

to consideration for the interest of the victim in a trial

free from unreasonable delay;

to an order of restitution from the convicted offender;

to consideration for the safety of the victim in determining any release from custody; and

to reasonable notice of the rights established by this article.

SECTION 2. Only the victim or the victim's representative shall have standing to assert the rights established by this article. Nothing in this article shall provide grounds for the victim to challenge a charging decision or a conviction; to overturn a sentence or negotiated plea; to obtain a stay of trial; or to compel a new trial. Nothing in this article shall give rise to a claim for damages against the United States, a State, a political subdivision, or a public official. . . .

SECTION 5. The rights established by this article shall apply in all Federal and State proceedings, including military proceedings to the extent that Congress may provide by law, juvenile justice proceedings, and proceedings in any district or territory of the United States not within a State.

In its 1998 incarnation, the amendment won the immediate support of 41 U.S. senators (26 short of the two-thirds majority necessary for passage), including such influential legislators as Majority Leader Trent Lott and Joseph Biden, the former chairman of the Senate Judiciary Committee. Substantial support also existed in the House of Representatives, though again it appeared short of a two-thirds majority. The amendment was also endorsed by President Clinton.

However, some victims' advocacy groups refused to support the amendment because they believed it had been watered down too much. The National Victim Center objected to two items in particular: making the amendment apply only to victims of violent crime (Section 1) and including language that would prevent victims from having a sentence or negotiated plea overturned because of violations of their rights (Section 2), which the center believed would essentially leave victims powerless. In a document explaining its opposition, the center indicated that there was no reason to compromise on key points because it was unlikely that the 105th Congress would pass the amendment anyway. And time, the center declared, was on the side of the victims' rights movement, which has been growing stronger with each passing year.

VICTIMS' RIGHTS . . . OR LEGAL WRONGS?

Richard Thornton (left), shown here with his daughter Katheryn Thornton and stepson William Davis, spoke forcefully for the execution of Karla Faye Tucker, his estranged wife Deborah's killer. Deborah Thornton's brother Ronald Carlson spoke just as forcefully against the execution. Who may invoke victims' rights and when can lead to some perplexing questions.

In the weeks leading up to the scheduled execution of Karla Faye Tucker, a heated public debate raged. At issue: whether the state of Texas should go ahead and put the 38-year-old convict to death for the gruesome crime she and a partner had committed some 15 years earlier. In addition to the general arguments in support of or against capital punishment, the Tucker case occasioned a public disagreement between two men with a more personal stake in the matter: former brothers-in-law Richard Thornton and Ronald Carlson.

On the night of June 13, 1983, Tucker and her accomplice, Daniel Garrett, had broken into the Houston apartment of an acquaintance, Jerry Lynn Dean, in order to steal some motorcycle parts they knew he had. Surprised to find Dean at home, they attacked him, Garrett hitting him on the head with a hammer and Tucker stabbing him more than 20 times with a pickax. After they had killed Dean, Garrett and Tucker noticed

33

his companion, 32-year-old Deborah Ruth Thornton, hiding under the covers of the bed, and they killed her too, leaving the pickax stuck in her abdomen. Deborah Thornton was the estranged wife of Richard Thornton and the sister of Ronald Carlson.

There was little sympathy for Tucker, a drug addict and prostitute, at the time of her trial. She freely admitted to killing the victims; indeed, she claimed that each blow with the pickax had given her sexual pleasure. Tucker was convicted of murder and sentenced to death, as was Garrett.

Garrett died of liver disease before he could be executed, but in the years she spent on death row, Tucker underwent a dramatic—and evidently sincere—transformation. Before her arrest, she had been a wild, angry, violent person. At a young age she had been forced into prostitution by her mother and was addicted to drugs. In prison she became a born-again Christian. Soft-spoken and thoughtful, she spent much of her time trying to help other inmates. In short, she seemed rehabilitated.

Ronald Carlson, Deborah Thornton's brother, believed that Karla Faye Tucker's life should be spared, and he worked hard to get her death sentence commuted. She was a different person now, Carlson argued, from the 23-year-old who had killed his sister. Richard Thornton, on the other hand, insisted that the execution proceed; justice for his wife demanded that the state carry out the sentence decided upon by the jury, he said. The case raised some interesting questions. Which of the two men—both family members of the victim—had the superior claim to be heard and heeded? Should the fact that he and his wife were separated at the time of her death lessen Thornton's standing to speak for her?

The Tucker case points to one of the pitfalls of centralizing victims' concerns in criminal justice: defining who is a victim and who has standing to exercise victims' rights can be much more problematic than one might think. And what happens when two victims of the same offender have different views on how to exercise their rights? Should the state try to balance the wishes of the victims? Should a poll be taken of all the family members of a murder victim?

To those who view victims' rights skeptically, it really shouldn't matter what *anybody* in the victim's family thinks about the appropriate punishment. Once a crime has been committed, the punishment lies between the offender and the state, not between the victim or the victim's survivors and the state. And in order to be fair, the state must be painstakingly careful

Predictors of Victimization

Who are victims? The answer to this question, while short and obvious, is still problematic. Anyone can be a crime victim, at any time, at any place. Yet accepting this as an intellectual proposition and really believing it are two different matters. To a great degree, our ability to function normally hinges on our feelings of safety and security. A person acutely aware of the possibility that he or she could be violently attacked at any moment—while walking down the street, talking in a school hallway, riding a bus, sitting at the kitchen table—would find it extremely difficult to get through the day. So even though most of us acknowledge that crime can happen at any time to anybody, people usually seem genuinely shocked when they are victimized. "I didn't think this could happen to me" is a common statement heard from crime victims. The first casualty of victimization is often one's sense of security, and victims frequently have trouble adjusting to a more realistic view of how vulnerable they really are.

While everyone is vulnerable to crime, the people who report the most crimes are young males. This is probably because young men are most likely to be out in public at night and most likely to fight with one another. Statistically, a good predictor of future victimization is the level of a person's fear of crime. This is not because being afraid causes people to be attacked, but because people tend to be good judges of whether or not they are in risky situations. A woman who works nights in a high-crime area and walks home alone is understandably more likely to be afraid of assaults than is a woman who works during daylight hours in a low-crime area.

An even better predictor of future victimization is whether a person has been victimized before. This is true even though previous victims, as a group, are neither more nor less cautious than the general population. Rather, a person who is often in a situation in which he or she is victimized (for example, a woman married to a man who assaults her) is likely to be in that situation again.

to safeguard the procedures used against individual offenders. (In the case of Karla Faye Tucker, the state did, ultimately, have the final word. The Texas Board of Pardons and Paroles denied Tucker's bid for clemency, and Governor George W. Bush refused to stay the execution. Tucker died by lethal injection on February 3, 1998.)

Fairness also dictates that offenders who commit identical crimes receive at least somewhat similar punishment, and opponents of victims' rights believe that allowing victims to be heard at various points in a criminal proceeding could undermine this goal. This remains a concern, they say, even with the 1998 version of the proposed victims' rights constitutional

Who Can Invoke Victims' Rights?

States typically extend victims' rights to the direct victims of violent crime and, in cases of murder, to surviving members of the victim's family. As the Karla Faye Tucker case demonstrates, this isn't always as straightforward as it sounds. *Arizona v. Coronado,* a case decided in 1996, dealt with another perplexing victims' rights scenario.

Arizona's victims' bill of rights provides, among other things, that a victim cannot be ordered to give interviews to the defendant's lawyers or representatives. This right is extended to direct victims of crimes and sometimes to their families. Normally, when people have important information about an alleged crime, they can be subpoenaed (ordered to appear in court) and forced to tell the judge or jury what they know. Even though the right to interview people with information is crucial to mounting an effective defense, Arizona is willing to suspend that right rather than put a victim through the trauma of having to cooperate with the defendant (and possibly helping him make his case). Arizona's victims' bill of rights also specifies that a deceased victim's family does not have to cooperate with the defense. In *Arizona v. Coronado,* that protection was invoked by the parents of a sexual assault victim who committed suicide between the time of the attack and the trial of the accused.

The defendant was not accused of murdering the woman, so his lawyers felt that they should be allowed to interview her parents. But the prosecutor, and subsequently the state of Arizona, maintained that the victim's suicide was related to the earlier assault, so the woman's parents were entitled to exercise their right not to cooperate with the defense counsel. At issue was whether Arizona's victims' bill of rights covered the family of any deceased victim or whether it applied only when the victim died as a *direct result* of the defendant's alleged crimes.

amendment, which eliminated provisions that would have enabled victims to reject plea bargains. The basic problem, critics say, is that some victims will take every opportunity to be heard—at bail hearings, during plea hearings, during sentencing, even at parole hearings—while others will take no interest in exercising their victims' rights. The likelihood, therefore, is that some defendants will end up being much more severely punished than others who committed identical crimes simply because of the involvement of their victims in the legal process. And, because prosecutors aren't immune from pressure, defendants whose victims are particularly vocal at the early stages of a criminal proceeding might even be more likely to be charged

The Court of Appeals of Arizona held that "only if the deceased is killed by the alleged criminal offenses with which the defendant is charged" can his or her family refuse to be interviewed by defense lawyers. Further, in the particular case at hand, the connection between the earlier sexual assault and the subsequent suicide was too speculative for the woman's parents to be considered victims within the meaning of the law. Therefore the defendant could not be deprived of his right to question them.

Looked at from the point of view of the parents, this outcome would seem unfair, particularly if they believed that the defendant committed the assault. In their minds two horrible things happened because of the offender: first their daughter was sexually assaulted, then she killed herself. They might see themselves as doubly victimized by the defendant, and therefore twice as entitled to the protection afforded by Arizona's victims' bill of rights.

If the accused were truly innocent of the sexual assault, however, one way to convince the court of his innocence would be to show why his accuser could not be believed. Perhaps she was mentally unstable and imagined that things happened when they really did not. The fact that she chose to take her own life could be a sign of mental disturbance. If she had a history of suicide attempts or of making false accusations, that information could be crucial to the defense—and directly questioning her parents might be the only way to uncover it.

One's opinion of the case likely changes depending on whose point of view one considers—and even more, depending on whether or not the defendant is really presumed innocent until proven guilty in a court of law, as American criminal procedure dictates. For if the defendant is extended the presumption of innocence, then it is difficult to justify hampering his ability to prepare his defense.

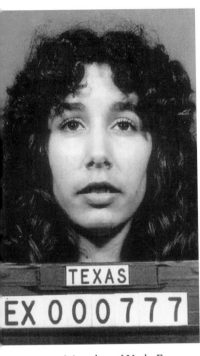

Mug shot of Karla Faye Tucker, 1983. Nearly 15 years later, on February 3, 1998, the state of Texas executed the convicted murderer.

with more-serious offenses and less likely to be offered a plea agreement.

While conceding that some inequities could result from this situation, victims' rights advocates say the alternative, denying victims the right to participate, would be much more unfair. First of all, victims have done nothing wrong. Second, many factors in the criminal justice system can lead to vastly different outcomes for defendants who have committed identical crimes—the skill of their lawyers and of the district attorneys who prosecute them, for example. There is a principle in civil law holding that you take your victim as you find him. If you are sued by someone who slips and falls on the ice in front of your house, and that person has very brittle bones, you cannot argue that it is unfair that you have to pay for many broken bones. Similarly, many victims' rights advocates would argue, the chance that the person you victimize will tenaciously pursue his or her rights is a risk you assume when you choose to commit a crime in the first place.

But opponents of the victims' rights amendment see an even more fundamental danger than the possibility that identical crimes will be punished vastly differently. They see a threat to one of the hallowed foundations of American justice: the presumption that the defendant is innocent until proven guilty in a court of law. Allowing a victim the right to be heard before the defendant's guilt has been established—indeed, before it has even been established that a crime was committed—could undermine the ability of the accused to get a fair trial. In testimony before the Senate Judiciary Committee, Elisabeth Semel, director and cochair of the Legislative Committee of the National Association of Criminal Defense Lawyers, summed up the subtle dynamic of this situation: "[The amendment] gives complaining witnesses the 'victim' label, so the accused immediately becomes the 'victim's' symbolic opposite, 'the perpetrator,' *at the inception of the criminal justice proceedings—upon mere accusation."*

The Constitution takes extraordinary measures to protect the rights of the accused precisely because these people stand alone against the powerful state—and, in many cases, against a hostile community—with the possibility of losing their property, their liberty, or even their life in the process. The addition of victims to the already formidable powers arrayed against the accused in legal proceedings would, critics say, tip the balance too far toward the state. And the inevitable result, they say, would be more cases decided on emotion rather than reason, and an infinitely greater risk of wrongful convictions.

In addition to their concerns about the impact on the rights of the accused, critics point to various practical problems with victims' rights. Under the terms of the proposed constitutional amendment, for example, victims have the right to appear in court and be heard at least three times during a criminal case: "during proceedings to determine a release from custody, an acceptance of a negotiated plea, or a sentence." They also have the right to "reasonable notice" of these proceedings. Typically, a release from custody, acceptance of a negotiated plea, and sentencing take place on three separate occasions: at a bail hearing, at a settlement conference, and at sentencing, respectively. However, the legal process is notoriously unpredictable. Many misdemeanor cases are completely resolved at arraignment (the defendant's first appearance in court) when the defendant enters a guilty plea and is sentenced immediately. Many felony cases are also settled unexpectedly at motion hearings, which are hearings intended to iron out various legal questions before the actual trial begins. Because victims would be entitled to reasonable notice of a proposed plea agreement and sentencing, such quick and cost-effective settlements would be impossible, and courts whose dockets are already full would face an added burden.

SEARCHING
FOR CLOSURE

Not surprisingly, victims tend to view crime and punishment somewhat differently from lawyers and criminal defendants. For them, legal concerns, such as the need to protect the rights of accused offenders, may take a backseat to personal concerns, such as how they can put their ordeal behind them and get on with their lives. Many victims view the criminal justice system—specifically, seeing the offender found guilty and punished—as providing their best opportunity for healing and closure. For survivors of murder victims, this may mean seeing the perpetrator executed. Such is the case with brother and sister Brooks and Leslie Douglass.

On October 15, 1979, between the hours of 7:45 and 10:00 P.M., Marilyn Douglass, the Reverend Richard Douglass, and their two children, 16-year-old Brooks and 12-year-old Leslie, were brutally attacked in their home. Steven Keith Hatch and Glen Burton Ake tricked the Douglass family into letting them into their

Leslie and Brooks Douglass, photographed during the 1980 trial of their parents' killers. At the time, the Douglass children could hardly have suspected that what lay ahead was a 16-year odyssey through the criminal justice system, during which they would be compelled to publicly revisit their horrible victimization at seven different hearings.

house in Okarche, Oklahoma, a rural town about 25 miles northwest of Oklahoma City. At the time, Steven Hatch was 26 years old and Glen Ake was 24. The two men had just quit their oil-rigging jobs and gone on a drug and alcohol binge. Hatch and Ake had already bothered a family in a nearby house when they randomly selected the Douglass home. Ake knocked on the door first, pretending he was lost; he said he was looking for someone named "Mitchell" who lived in the area. Brooks Douglass offered to let him use the telephone. Ake said he needed to go back to his car to get Mitchell's telephone number, but when he returned he had a gun with him. Hatch barged through the front door as well, also with a gun. After tying up the Reverend and Mrs. Douglass and Brooks, they made Leslie bring them all the money, jewelry, and credit cards she could find. Then they dragged her into a bedroom and sexually molested her, brought her back out, and tied her up with the rest of the family.

Ake and Hatch stayed in the Douglasses' house for well over two hours. During that time they sat down and ate the family's dinner, which was already set out on the table. Brooks says that the family could hear them eating and talking about killing their victims. According to Ake, he finally told Hatch to go outside, turn the car around, and listen for the sound of gunfire. Ake proceeded to shoot all four of the Douglasses (each of whom was still lying on the living room floor, tied hand and foot) in the back. The Reverend and Mrs. Douglass bled to death, but the two youngsters survived their gunshot wounds. Thirty-seven days later, Ake and Hatch were arrested.

The aftermath of this attack was devastating to Brooks and Leslie Douglass. In order to support them, their family's home and most of their belongings were sold off at an auction less than a month after the murders. They were both hospitalized (Brooks was shot once, Leslie twice) and missed their parents' funeral because they were too weak to attend. They were separated, so besides losing their parents they essentially lost each other as well. Brooks was in his senior year (a successful student, he had skipped 11th grade), and he stayed with friends in Okarche to complete high school. Leslie was sent to live with cousins in another city in Oklahoma.

Symptoms of Victimization

The victim of a violent crime may suffer physical injury and financial costs (in the form of medical bills and lost wages), but the most painful and lingering effects may be psychological damage. The symptoms do not necessarily manifest themselves right away. Indeed, the immediate response to a violent assault is often numbness and shock. A person who has been attacked may appear unusually calm, but this does not mean that he or she hasn't been profoundly affected by the ordeal.

The list of psychological symptoms suffered by the victims of violent crimes is long, and obviously not all victims suffer all of these difficulties. Still, there is a great consistency among victims of violent crime in reporting the following problems: depression, terror, rage, sleep difficulties, heightened response to stimuli, agoraphobia (fear and avoidance of public places), panic attacks, psychosomatic complaints (symptoms that have no physical cause), and difficulties in close relationships. Although it seems illogical, victims frequently feel anxiety, guilt, and shame. A violent assault can have extremely profound effects on a person, attacking his or her very sense of self, including self-esteem, identity, and feelings of safety and personal integrity.

Psychologists agree that the extent to which victims suffer from the above is based on the interplay of personal and situational details. The following four factors largely determine a victim's emotional injury:

1. *The nature and extent of the violence suffered.* The more violent and disfiguring the assault, the more actual life changes the victim must cope with and confront.

2. *The victim's previous relationship with the offender.* If the violence was perpetrated by someone the victim loved and trusted, that betrayal causes many emotional problems in addition to those of the assault itself.

3. *The location of the crime.* Being attacked in one's home, workplace, or any place where one is used to feeling safe and secure can have a huge impact on one's sense of personal safety (more so than if one is assaulted on the street).

4. *The victim's emotional condition before the crime occurred.* People who were emotionally fragile or unusually dependent before they were violently assaulted will probably have a more severe response to their victimization.

Steven Hatch, convicted in the 1979 murder of Richard and Marilyn Douglass, pleads his case at a clemency hearing, July 1996.

Brooks Douglass frequently points out that the terrible crime has dominated his and his sister's lives. "It has affected all of the decisions in my life," he reports. "No one should have to spend their life dealing with something that happened when they were sixteen years old." Brooks and Leslie testified in detail at seven different hearings, and according to Brooks his anger and sense of loss only intensified with each court appearance. Brooks says that testifying was increasingly painful. "[E]very time it got harder. The numbness wears off. . . . As I got older, I became angrier over the loss, angrier that I would have to disrupt my life."

Leslie also talks about how difficult recovering from the crime has been. "It never gets any better, only worse. You're sitting there in your spouse's house for the holidays with all the family and your kids, and it's as lonely as it can be. . . . You end up asking yourself 'is my whole life going to be like this? Is my life doomed . . . ?'"

Both Leslie and Brooks say they were relieved when Hatch and Ake were sentenced to death in 1980. But Ake's death sentence was later overturned and reduced to two life sentences because of a very important legal principle. Ake had wanted to plead insanity as a defense, but he couldn't afford a psychiatrist to help him prepare his case. There was evidence that he might be mentally ill. In fact, his behavior in court was so bizarre that the judge ordered Ake to undergo tests to determine whether he was competent to stand trial. He was found not so and was returned for trial only after he had been heavily medicated for 60 days. Unfortunately for Ake, this evidence spoke to his mental state at the time of trial but was not sufficient to prove his mental state at the time he committed the crimes. Although Ake was unable to prepare an insanity defense, the state managed to use his mental illness against him, arguing that it increased his "future dangerousness," which in Oklahoma constitutes an aggravating factor (a factor that calls for harsher punishment). In other words, while the jury could not consider Ake's mental illness as a reason to punish him less severely, they were asked to use it as a reason to punish him more severely. Ake appealed his case all the way to the United States Supreme Court, which ruled that the denial of psychiatric assistance meant Ake had been denied a fair trial.

Although he struggled for a while and had problems settling down, Brooks Douglass ultimately went to college, completed law school, and became a state senator in Oklahoma. Brooks strongly believed that having Hatch put to death would be the best way for him and his sister to finish healing. "When Steven Hatch is executed, I know the door to that part of my life will be closed. . . . The death penalty is the ultimate closure. It is the ultimate sign that it is over, that there are no more possibilities that my life will be debilitated by reliving the crime, no more possibilities that this man will get out and do to someone else what he did to my family." As a member of the state legislature, Douglass wrote a bill allowing the family members of murder victims to be present at the execution of any person convicted of killing their relative. Previously, family members were allowed to be in the prison during an execution and to watch the execution via video.

Brooks Douglass successfully steered his bill through Oklahoma's state legislature, making Oklahoma the eighth state to allow victims' relatives to be present at executions. On August 9, 1996, Brooks, his sister Leslie, and three of their uncles (their mother's brothers) watched through glass as Steven Hatch received a lethal injection in an adjoining chamber.

Victimization, Blame, and the Desire for Control

For reasons that are hard to grasp for people who have not been violently assaulted, crime victims suffer a serious attack on their own sense of self-worth. Victims almost always want to project meaning onto their horrible experience, and one way to achieve that is to project personal responsibility onto the crime. It may not make sense at first, but if you think that you did something to cause your victimization, then you must have had some control over it, and you can therefore prevent the victimization from happening again.

The desire to have had control over a horrible event is counterintuitive, but when a battered wife says that she caused her abuse by burning dinner, she is trying, in part, to convince herself that as long as she never burns dinner again she will never be assaulted again.

Victims do not blame themselves in a vacuum. The inclination to blame oneself is reinforced by the tendency of other people to blame the victim, too. Like the person attacked, others want to convince themselves that the victim had some responsibility for and control over the assault. This allows them to fool themselves into thinking that such an awful thing could never happen to them.

The most obvious example of an innocent, helpless group of victims might be child victims of

Brooks Douglass made a public statement after the execution, saying, "We're very sad and very sorry that the circumstances of seventeen years ago have brought us to this place. Leslie and I have again witnessed the taking of a life. The first time we did, we were young people who were present when our mother and father were viciously killed. It is the end of a very long ordeal that has dominated our lives."

Hatch left a typed note discussing his upcoming execution, in which he called "those who sit in judgment . . . evil and barbaric."

When they were told about the note, Leslie and Brooks thought it confirmed their opinion of Hatch. Leslie said, "It was appalling—we were just horrified. But he has allowed me to never doubt what he is. He had no remorse. I just sat there watching him die and feeling so much anger that he was able to go peacefully. All I kept thinking about was how I laid hog-tied, with my face buried in a carpet, praying that I would live." Brooks said, "I'll let others draw their own con-

father-daughter incest. These victims cannot blame themselves for being in the wrong place at the wrong time, since they are attacked in their homes. Nor can they second-guess their judgment of character, since they have no control over who their parents are. Nevertheless, a survey study showed that many of these victims engage in a long-term struggle with the problem of making sense of what happened to them. They are not necessarily looking for a way to blame themselves or anyone else. They simply feel a strong need to search for an explanation for their attacks.

The authors of the study point out that psychologists believe constantly thinking about something, or trying to explain it to oneself, is the mind's way to gain a kind of control over the event. Without blaming themselves, or excusing the abusive adult, some victims focus on the dynamics that allowed the incest to occur: their father's character flaws or mental illness, their mother's absence or estrangement, or the situation in their homes at the time. Some victims seem to resolve this problem by accepting that it is impossible to figure out. Others try to extract a positive lesson from the horrible experience, concluding that nothing as bad as the incest will ever happen to them again, and that in surviving that ordeal they have proven that there is virtually nothing they cannot overcome.

While his sister Leslie dabs a tear, Brooks Douglass listens to testimony at Steven Hatch's clemency hearing. According to Brooks Douglass, he and Leslie wanted the criminal justice system to allow them to get on with their lives, to provide closure to "years of anger and hate." When Hatch was finally executed, the Douglasses watched from a witness room reserved for victims' family members.

clusions about his final message. All I can do is deal with my own feelings. I will say that I wished he had surprised me in some way."

In an essay published a few months before Hatch's execution, Brooks Douglass had emphasized the healing he hoped to achieve by watching his parents' murderer put to death.

It is not retaliation or retribution that I seek in witnessing the execution of the man who killed my parents. It is closure. Closure on an era of my life into which I never chose to enter. Closure of years of anger and hate. . . . Ideally the criminal justice system should be to punish the offenders while allowing the victim to go on with his life. . . . I was never once allowed to tell the jury anything but the facts. The jury never heard of the struggles I faced in life because I didn't have parents. I was never able to tell what it feels like to spend the holidays alone. . . . As a senator, I wanted to work for a criminal justice system that's fair to defendants and victims and that allows victims the chance to move on with their lives.

Douglass argued for the use of victim impact statements as a way to help victims find closure:

In the sentencing phase, victims or their families testify about the crime's emotional, psychological and physical effects. Testifying gives the victim a chance to be heard. Voicing these feelings allows the victim to feel a part of and in turn accept the outcome of the process. . . . Once the victim believes justice is served, the victim can find closure. Closure is something each person must find for himself. I can't prescribe treatment, nor can I legislate it.

Both Brooks and Leslie reported feeling the closure they had hoped for immediately after the execution. "I do believe that it's the end of a very long ordeal that's dominated our lives," Brooks stated. "I'm just glad that I hadn't ignored the rest of my life all these years because I would be very disappointed today. He's gone, it's over. I can get back to my law practice, my family."

Leslie said, "I don't know if it will last, but I feel great today. I feel people care and feel my parents are at peace. . . . I can move on. I can focus on my children."

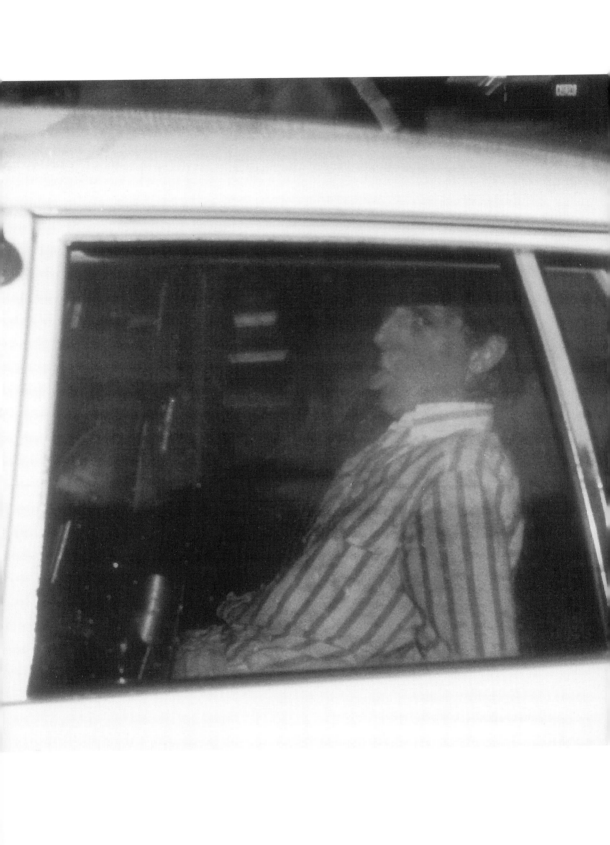

LETTING GO
OF THE ANGER

When Nancy and Richard Langert returned to their townhouse in Winnetka, Illinois, after having dinner with Nancy's parents on April 7, 1990, they found a 16-year-old high school junior waiting for them. The boy, David Biro, had a gun, and at some point in the evening he bound Richard Langert's hands. Apparently the couple spent quite a bit of time negotiating with him, trying to convince him to take whatever he wanted, including their CD player and several hundred dollars in cash, but to leave them unhurt. After a while, the teenager ordered the Langerts into the basement. First he shot Richard Langert, 30, in the back of the head, and when Nancy, who was 25 years old and three months pregnant, tried to run up the stairs, he shot her three times: in the elbow, back, and abdomen. Then

High school student David Biro reacts to his arrest for the murders of Richard and Nancy Langert.

Biro left the Langerts' townhouse without taking any of their belongings.

It is obvious that Nancy Langert lived for a while, since she crawled over to her husband's body and tried to write something on the floor with his blood. Her family believes she tried to draw a heart and write "I love you." This interpretation is important to them because, as Nancy's sister Jeanne Bishop pointed out, "In the last moments of her life, Nancy left a message of love." At the end of their defense case, Biro's lawyers disputed this. They argued that she was really trying to write the name "Burke." They claimed their client was innocent and that the blood spelled out the name of the person who really shot the Langerts. Nobody knows with certainty what Nancy was trying to write because she died before she could finish.

The police had a lot of trouble figuring out what had happened to the Langerts. There was no robbery, and Nancy's parents and her two sisters could not think of any enemies the couple had. One of Nancy's sisters, Jeanne Bishop, was very active in Irish politics, and the police spent much time investigating her and her connections, wondering if someone had killed Nancy and her husband as a way to hurt or intimidate Jeanne. They also focused on the business Nancy and Richard worked for, explored possible drug use and mob con-

Effect of Victimization on Sense of Security

Lynne Henderson argues that the victim's sudden and unexpected confrontation with his or her own mortality is by far the most traumatic aspect of violent crime. All at once isolation, feelings of insignificance, and a profound fear of death combine to have far-reaching and devastating psychological consequences. The primary experience of victimization is the lack of control the victim endures during the crime. To victims this lack of control may seem to extend past the actual crime, and in their own lives they no longer feel they exercise any significant autonomy. They no longer feel "at home" in the world. Their sense of security and safety are stripped away so that everything seems unfamiliar and somehow threatening.

nections, and looked into the couple's personal lives, including an unhappy period in their marriage. The investigation was very painful for everyone involved but yielded no promising suspects.

David Biro didn't come to the attention of police for a long time. After several months, however, he began to tell other kids at his high school that he had committed the murders. He seemed to be trying to impress them, but most of his classmates gave his story no credence. Finally, though, one of his friends went to the police and reported that Biro had described the murders. According to the friend, Biro said he had cut glass panes out of the patio doors, then waited for the Langerts to come home. He claimed that the Langerts had begged for their lives, and that Nancy had especially pleaded for the life of her baby. Biro said he had offered to lock the Langerts in the basement and then leave but that on the way downstairs Nancy Langert saw his face. Fearing she would be able to identify him, he decided he had to kill them both. Biro, the friend said, had even shown him the murder weapon. Finally, on October 5, 1990, almost six months to the day after the murders, David Biro was arrested.

When police searched his bedroom, they found a pair of glass cutters and two sets of handcuffs that were consistent with the marks found on Richard Langert's wrists. They also found a .357 Magnum hidden under Biro's bed. It was the gun that had been used to kill the Langerts.

At his trial David Biro admitted that he had talked to the police informant and other students at New Trier High School about the killings, but he maintained that he was only kidding around. He said that except for the student who went to the police, all the other teenagers had known it was a joke. Biro had a convoluted story to explain why he had the murder weapon. He testified that he had stolen the gun from his lawyer's office and had then given it to a classmate named Burke so the classmate could sell it. But Burke never sold the gun; instead, he returned it on the night of April 7, telling Biro to hide it because the gun had just been used to kill two people.

In November of 1991, when he was 18 years old, David Biro was convicted of murdering Richard and Nancy Langert and of killing Nancy Langert's fetus. The jury took only two hours to reach its verdict. Several jurors said they could not believe Biro's story about how he had come to possess the murder weapon. Because he was only 16 at the time he committed the murders, Biro was not eligible for the death penalty. But Illinois law required that he be sentenced to life in prison without possibility of parole because he was convicted of more than one murder.

The most troubling aspect of this crime was the complete lack of motive on the part of the 16-year-old. When the judge sentenced Biro, he said, "It wasn't a killing for profit. It wasn't a killing because of any threatened action by the decedents. It was simply a cold-blooded killing. He wanted to kill apparently to achieve some sort of infamy from that killing—some sort of notoriety for that killing."

Nancy's family was especially bothered by the senselessness of the crime. Jeanne Bishop, Nancy's sister, said, "I think we all wished that part of his sentence would be that he sit down with us and tell us why. How could you do this?" She felt that the anger and frustration borne of never knowing Biro's reasons (or having to accept that in fact he had none) "is part of our life sentence, I suppose." Jeanne was grateful for the guilty verdict, explaining, "Nothing is going to bring her back. But at least we know the person responsible is going to be held accountable." Nancy's father, Lee Bishop, said simply, "I don't have my children back."

Jeanne Bishop and Nancy's other sister, Jennifer Jones, became active in a group called Murder Victims' Families for Reconciliation. The group is a national

network that works, among other things, against the death penalty. Murder Victims' Families for Reconciliation warns victims against hoping that with the execution of the offender they will achieve emotional satisfaction and psychological healing, or that the execution will offer them a sense of closure and justice. Rather, Murder Victims' Families for Reconciliation asserts that the better way to heal and a more genuine satisfaction is derived from the repudiation of rage toward the offender.

To the members of Murder Victims' Families for Reconciliation, "reconciliation" does not mean that the families of murder victims are expected to become friendly with the murderers. Instead, the word "means letting go of those things that keep you from healing. It means reconciling your life to a change that you can't

Nancy Langert's sister, Jeanne Bishop (right), along with her mother, Joyce. Jeanne Bishop is active in Murder Victims' Families for Reconciliation, a group that advises victims to let go of their rage against the criminal—for their own sake.

undo." They do not think that horrible crimes should be forgotten or ignored. They do not encourage people to specifically forgive or reconcile with the person who committed a brutal crime. Rather, the members of the group, all of whom have lost people they loved to murder, think families need to reconcile themselves to the sadness and injustice of losing a parent or sibling or child. Then they need to learn to let go of the anger and rage that can consume their families.

For example, even though both of Nancy Langert's sisters are members of Murder Victims' Families for Reconciliation, Nancy's family has no relationship with David Biro. He has never apologized or attempted to reach out to the Bishops. Yet Jennifer Jones said that her and her sister Jeanne's search for inner peace and reconciliation let them have closure at Biro's sentencing. This, she argues, is better than spending year after year pursuing the offender through the criminal justice system and hoping to see him or her killed. The extreme tension and emotional pain that comes with that kind of struggle is a considerable burden that, according to Murder Victims' Families for Reconciliation, victims' families would do better not to assume. When they argue for reconciliation, it is not for the offender's sake, but for the family's sake.

Constance Mitchell, another member of Murder Victims' Families for Reconciliation, suffered a tragic loss when her son and cousin were murdered during a grocery robbery. When she and Jennifer Jones made an appearance to speak on behalf of her son's killer, she said that withdrawing from vengeance and violence is "the [only] way you can be healed. You can't spend the rest of your life grieving and hating. You have to find the peace that was taken from you. . . . Hate in the heart will never do anyone any good."

Marie Deans, the founder of Murder Victims' Families for Reconciliation, knows that people who commit horrible crimes are not formed in a vacuum, and they

do not develop their problems overnight. "I have yet to find a case," she says,

> where there wasn't a red flag thrown up years ago—in grammar school or somewhere—where a kid said, "I'm in trouble, help me." He gave us the message loud and clear and we didn't pay any attention. And he ended up years later, going down and down and killing someone. Let me tell you something. I resent the hell out of that as a member of a murder victim's family. . . . These governors, these prosecutors . . . all getting up and saying, "I care about victims, I want the death penalty." If they cared about victims, they would have taken care of that victimized kid when he was six years old and prevented a homicide later.

Reconciliation is not on the minds of these young men, who are showing their support for the execution of convicted murderer Westley Allan Dodd.

Deans knows that it is difficult, if not impossible, to sympathize with people like Steven Hatch, Glen Ake, and David Biro at the time they committed their brutal crimes. Her argument is that very likely there was a time, probably long before they murdered, when they were in serious need of help and they did not get it. If someone had just reached out to them then, she believes, that person would not only have made Biro's, Ake's, and Hatch's lives more productive, but also, possibly, saved the lives of Richard and Nancy Langert and Richard and Marilyn Douglass.

People like Marie Deans, Constance Mitchell, and Nancy Langert's two sisters, Jennifer Jones and Jeanne Bishop, feel that they can be particularly effective proponents of this viewpoint, since they themselves have suffered the pain felt by murder victims' families. No one can accuse them of not knowing what it feels like to have a loved one killed or of being insensitive to the concerns and needs of people going through a horrible ordeal. Their emphasis is on the peace that came to their lives after they had progressed beyond the anger and desire for revenge that was their initial reaction. As Constance Mitchell put it, the person who murdered her son and cousin did a terrible thing, "[b]ut I had to forgive him for my own sake."

Jennifer Jones, Jeanne Bishop, and other members of Murder Victims' Families for Reconciliation have had very different reactions to their painful experiences than did Brooks and Leslie Douglass. The Douglasses seemed to pin their hopes for closure on the criminal justice system while at the same time finding the criminal justice system itself a source of continuing pain. Brooks Douglass complained about having to testify on repeated occasions, which reopened all his wounds, but in another respect he seemed to want to participate in the system more than he was allowed to. In an interview he talked about wanting to testify about the murders, but when he took the stand, all the lawyers asked him to do was identify the jewelry his mother was wearing the night she was murdered. Inevitably, what is most important to a surviving victim (how brave his mother was during the attack, or the way she cooked lasagna, or sang a certain song) will never be most important to the court system. And there are limits to the psychic satisfaction one can hope to derive from seeing the offender punished. Some defendants will not get the sentence their victims think they deserve. In the case of Brooks and Leslie Douglass, the man who actually pulled the trigger and killed their parents, Glen Ake, will never be executed. Whatever gains the victims' rights movement makes, it is doubtful that the criminal justice system will ever be an adequate vehicle for healing victims' pain. That is a goal it was simply not designed to achieve.

REJECTING VICTIM IMPACT STATEMENTS: BOOTH V. MARYLAND

The opportunity to inform the court about the personal impact a crime has had—to deliver a victim impact statement—is one of the more prominent, and controversial, victims' rights. For victims it may represent a chance to tell their story in an emotionally satisfying way or perhaps to heal or achieve closure. Many, particularly the families of murder victims, tell the judge or jury about the good qualities of their loved one and about how emotionally devastating losing him or her has been. Victim impact testimony can be utterly heartrending.

And that is precisely what makes it controversial. There is no disputing the fact that allowing victims

Their faces covered, Demetrius Gathers and another suspect in the assault and murder of Richard Haynes are led into a South Carolina police station. A prosecutor's references to religious articles the victim was carrying would become the focus of South Carolina v. Gathers, *a case in which the Supreme Court rejected the admissibility of statements about the victim's personal qualities during a capital sentencing hearing.*

to testify about the personal impact of a crime may negatively affect the offender's rights, because it gives the prosecution an additional chance to emphasize its case in a more emotional (and perhaps more persuasive) manner. The question is, are allowing the victim to be heard in court and protecting the constitutionally guaranteed rights of the accused always incompatible, and if not, under what circumstances is victim impact testimony permissible? To understand the issues, it is helpful to look at how trials for the most serious crimes are conducted.

Trials for crimes that can result in the death penalty are routinely divided into two stages. The first, the guilt phase, operates like any other trial, with the jury deciding whether or not the accused person actually committed the crime. If the defendant is found guilty, there is a second proceeding, the penalty phase, in which the sentencing authority—either the jury or judge—makes a different decision: whether, given that the offender is guilty, he or she should be put to death. During the penalty phase, the sentencer weighs two sets of factors: aggravating factors, which, if present, make a given crime more serious and warrant a stricter punishment, and mitigating factors, which, if present, make the offender less culpable. For example, many state laws specify that if a person kills a victim in exchange for money, the sentencing authority should consider that a reason to apply the death penalty. In contrast, a mitigating factor might be the offender's youth. During the penalty phase defendants typically call witnesses who try to personalize them for the judge or jury in an effort to get a more lenient sentence; victims, on the other hand, almost always make victim impact statements with the objective of convincing the judge or jury to sentence the defendant more harshly.

Defense lawyers argue that not only can victim impact statements be inflammatory and highly prejudicial, but they are also of questionable relevance.

Whether a murder victim was a beloved part of a large family or a lonely homeless person should have no effect on how severely the killer is punished because every life is of equal value. And yet victim impact statements do, opponents argue, increase the likelihood that people who commit similar crimes will receive arbitrarily dissimilar sentences. Furthermore, by centralizing the emotional trauma of direct victims or surviving family members in punishment decisions, these statements in effect signify a return to the blood-feud mentality; they promote the idea that the criminal justice system is supposed to be a vehicle for the victims' revenge.

Proponents of victim impact statements counter that fairness is the real issue. At sentencing the offender is allowed to introduce all manner of personal information in order to persuade the decision maker to lighten his or her punishment. If the sentencing authority is to be presented with a well-rounded picture of the defendant, complete with testimony from friends and family who try to personalize the offender, then it is only fair to let the victim or the victim's family have an opportunity to personalize the damage caused by the offender.

Most states and the federal government allow victim impact statements, either oral or written, under various circumstances. The Supreme Court has examined the constitutionality of victim impact evidence in several important cases, beginning in 1987. The Court first held victim impact statements to be unconstitutional in *Booth v. Maryland* (482 U.S. 496, 107 S.Ct. 2529). Four years later, in a stunning reversal, the Court upheld the use of victim impact statements in *Payne v. Tennessee* (501 U.S. 808).

The *Booth* case began in 1983, when John Booth and an accomplice named Willie Reich broke into the home of an elderly couple in Booth's West Baltimore neighborhood. The two men were hoping to steal money from the house, which belonged to Irvin and

Rose Bronstein, in order to buy heroin. When the robbers found the Bronsteins at home, however, they bound, gagged, and repeatedly stabbed the couple, killing them.

As part of its presentencing report after Booth's murder conviction, the Division of Parole and Probation included a victim impact statement. A Maryland statute required that the division collect information from the victim or the victim's family, and it further stipulated that the report could be read to the jury, or family members could be called to testify as to the information in the victim impact statement. The victim impact statement of the Bronsteins' son, daughter, son-in-law, and granddaughter included a description of the severe emotional impact of the crimes on the family; the personal characteristics of the victims; and the family members' opinions and characterizations of the crimes and of the offenders.

The statement conveyed a sense of how extraordinary the victims had been and provided a heartbreaking and eloquent description of the crime's consequences for their survivors. The Bronstein family was very close and loving, and Mr. and Mrs. Bronstein had been lively and energetic and had many friends. Their funeral was the largest in the history of the funeral home where it was held, and the family received over 1,000 sympathy cards, which they tried to answer personally. Irvin and Rose Bronstein's bodies were found two days before their granddaughter's wedding. Because their religion dictates that life and marriage are more important than death, the family went ahead with the ceremony, but, as might be imagined, it produced little joy.

The emotionally powerful victim impact statement wasn't written directly by the Bronsteins but was prepared by an employee of the Division of Parole and Probation, who added comments such as the following conclusion:

It became increasingly apparent to the writer as she talked to the family members that the murder of Mr. and Mrs. Bronstein is still such a shocking, painful, and devastating memory to them that it permeates every aspect of their daily lives. It is doubtful that they will ever be able to fully recover from this tragedy and not be haunted by the memory of the brutal manner in which their loved ones were murdered and taken from them. (482 U.S. 496 at 515)

Ultimately, John Booth was sentenced to death.

On appeal, lawyers for Booth argued that Maryland's statute allowing victim impact statements made the imposition of the death penalty so unpredictable and random that it violated the Eighth Amendment's ban on cruel and unusual punishment. (The Supreme Court had ruled, in the 1972 case of *Furman v. Georgia*, that the Eighth Amendment forbade the death penalty if it was "wantonly and freakishly imposed.") Booth's lawyers said that the emotionally charged thoughts and opinions about the crimes and the offenders yielded little or no relevant information but served only to distract and inflame the jury, keeping them from considering the relevant factors weighing for and against the defendant.

The lawyers for the state of Maryland defended the statute, and the death sentence of John Booth, by arguing that the emotional distress of the victims' family, and the victims' personal characteristics, were exactly the kinds of factors that the jury should have considered. Rather than being an irrelevant diversion, the state argued, the victim impact statement had been properly presented to and discussed by the sentencing jury. The state asserted that the jury ought to know more about the full extent of the impact upon the family and the severity of their loss. That way they would be better able to measure the seriousness of the offense.

Justice Lewis F. Powell delivered the majority opinion of the U.S. Supreme Court, which overturned Booth's death sentence. He acknowledged that while it

Justice Lewis F. Powell, who wrote the majority opinion in the 1987 case Booth v. Maryland, worried that allowing murder victims' families to testify about their grief or about their loved one's good character would in effect place a greater value on some lives than on others.

is often relevant and important for a jury to know the full range of consequences of an act before they can fairly punish an offender, in the case of capital crimes the rules are different. Because the decision to put someone to death is so important, juries faced with that decision are required to have an intense focus on the defendant as a "uniquely individual human bein[g]," Powell wrote, quoting from the 1976 Supreme Court case *Woodson v. North Carolina* (428 U.S. 280, 304). Powell did not say that the family's pain and grief were unimportant, but he insisted that in a death penalty case (more than in any other kind of trial), it is crucial that the jury focus exclusively on the defendant and his or her blameworthiness. Since most offenders do not know details about their victims, they cannot be making decisions based on how much pain they will cause the victims' families. Therefore, those factors are illegitimate in a sentencing hearing. The jury should consider only the defendant, his or her background, his or her record, and the circumstances of the crime.

Powell made the point that in some important ways, it really didn't matter how beloved the Bronsteins were:

> [I]n some cases the victim will not leave behind a family, or the family members may be less articulate in describing their feelings, even though their sense of loss is equally severe. The fact that the imposition of the death sentence may turn on such distinctions illustrates the danger of allowing juries to consider this information. Certainly the degree to which a family is willing and able to express its grief is irrelevant to the decision whether a defendant, who may merit the death penalty, should live or die. (482 U.S. 496, 505)

What if the Bronsteins didn't have any children or were fairly private people without many friends? Would that have made what John Booth did any *less* horrible? What if the Bronsteins had a big family but its members weren't good at describing how they felt or were too upset to talk about their loss? If the jury were to consider information about how popular a particular victim was, then it would in effect be saying that killing certain people is worse than killing others.

Focusing on the character of the victim would be another way of saying that some lives are worth more than others. Powell worried that if prosecutors began entering testimony about how wonderful a particular victim was, then it would only be fair if the defense were allowed to rebut, or disagree with, that testimony. Then defendants would want to be allowed to "put on evidence that the victim was of dubious moral character, was unpopular, or was ostracized from his family." This would *truly* be a way of putting the victim on trial.

Powell also rejected the other information included in the Bronsteins' victim impact statement. The family members' opinions of the crime and the offenders "can serve no other purpose than to inflame the jury and divert it from deciding the case on the relevant evidence concerning the crime and the defendant. As we have noted," he declared, citing the case of *Gardner v. Florida* (430 U.S. 349, 358), "any decision to impose the death sentence must 'be and appear to be, based on reason rather than caprice or emotion'" (482 U.S. 496, 508). Again, Powell emphasized the importance of limiting considerations to rational, relevant characteristics of the offender and his or her crime.

In a dissenting opinion, Justice Byron White explained why he hadn't voted with the majority. He emphasized that the state legislature had written the law allowing victim impact statements, and this decision was purely theirs to make. (It is not unusual for a judge to be concerned with the proper division of tasks among the three branches of government. Often, a judge will say that he or she does not necessarily like a particular law or support a particular concept but that this is irrelevant because it is the responsibility of the legislature to make laws.) White then proceeded to go over Powell's opinion, disagreeing, point by point, with

The specific harm a reckless driver causes is relevant to the decision on how severely that driver should be punished, Justice Byron White (facing page) pointed out in his dissent from the Booth decision. Similarly, White reasoned, the specific harm caused by a murderer is relevant, and the victim's family members should be allowed to inform the jury on that matter.

every argument the majority had made.

White's first point outlined his philosophical difference of opinion. In his view the impact on other people is relevant to assessing blameworthiness, and it is therefore a proper factor in sentencing decisions. He discusses a hypothetical example of two drivers who speed through a red light at the same intersection. The first happens not to hurt anybody, but the second, who is traveling at the same speed, kills a pedestrian. The

second driver, White observed, has caused more harm and should therefore be punished more severely than the first driver, even though the two did exactly the same thing. White declared that there is nothing unusual or unfair in a jury's wanting to know how much damage an offender caused and that this kind of evidence does go to blameworthiness and just punishment.

White came to the opposite conclusion from the majority in large part because of his second point. Unlike Powell and the four other justices who voted with him, White refused to acknowledge that death penalty cases are different from all other kinds of cases and that capital offenders deserve different treatment. "[I]f punishment can be enhanced in noncapital cases on the basis of the harm caused, irrespective of the offender's specific intention to cause such harm, I fail to see why the same approach is unconstitutional in death cases," he said (482 U.S. at 516-517). White referred to the defendant's right to be considered as a unique individual and asked why the victim should not also be considered as such.

White's third point addressed the idea that allowing victim impact statements creates the impression that

Post-Traumatic Stress Disorder

There are three major groups of symptoms of post-traumatic stress disorder, a psychological condition many victims of violent crime suffer from. First, there are persistent, intrusive, and distressing memories of the traumatic event. These may occur while the survivor sleeps, in the form of nightmares, or while he or she is awake, in the form of flashbacks. Flashbacks are more than unpleasant recollections of the event—which of course victims also have. Rather, during a flashback the victim actually relives, through a trick of the sensory system, the feelings of terror that he or she experienced at the time of the traumatic event.

The second group of symptoms involves the persistent avoidance of people, places, and things the victim associates with the trauma. A crime victim will likely want to withdraw from activities that arouse recollections of his or her victimization. A man assaulted in his home might decide to move rather than face constant reminders of his terrible experience. A woman assaulted at work or on her way home from work may decide to change her employment. The survivors of a homicide victim often report being unable even to drive by the home or workplace of their loved one.

Victims also avoid their own thoughts and feelings about the assault, which can make recovery extremely difficult. A person who is sexually assaulted may avoid sexual activities after the attack. Crime victims may experience detachment and estrangement from their friends and families, finding that they are unable to have loving feelings.

The third set of symptoms involves increased agitation or excitability. John Freedy and a number of social scientists wrote an article titled "The Psychological Adjustment of Recent Crime Victims in the Criminal Justice System." In this study they observed that crime victims frequently experience insomnia, irritability, and increased startle response (or jumpiness). Crime victims can have difficulty concentrating, and formerly easygoing people may start having outbursts of anger.

The symptoms of post-traumatic stress disorder tend to wax and wane over time, based on a combination of external events and the victim's personality, but they are usually chronic, and traces of this disorder are likely to last throughout one's life. It is important to note that the symptoms of post-traumatic stress disorder can also affect the "indirect" victims, or the loved ones of a person who is violently victimized.

A police officer helps a distraught woman at the scene of a 1984 shooting spree that claimed 20 lives. Victims of severe violence are likely to suffer from post-traumatic stress disorder, the symptoms of which may last a lifetime.

some lives are more worthy or valuable than others. While agreeing that it would be unconstitutional for the sentencer to rely on certain factors (such as the race of the victim), "I fail to see," he said, "why the State cannot, if it chooses, include as a sentencing consideration the particularized harm that an individual's murder causes to the rest of society and in particular to his family" (482 U.S. at 517).

White did not think Powell's fourth point, about unfairly advantaging more articulate family members, was persuasive. He pointed out that those kinds of variations and inequalities are widespread in the criminal justice system: "No two prosecutors have exactly

In a dissenting opinion in the case of South Carolina v. Gathers, *Justice Sandra Day O'Connor suggested that the victim needn't be reduced to a "faceless stranger" in capital sentencing decisions.*

the same ability to present their arguments to the jury; no two witnesses have exactly the same ability to communicate the facts. . . ." If variable persuasiveness of witnesses creates unconstitutional arbitrariness, then no trial can ever be fair. Of course, White could make this argument only because he had already rejected the majority's premise that death penalty cases are substantially different from all other kinds of cases, and therefore defendants are entitled to extra protection of their rights.

Finally, White addressed Powell's concern about the defendant's right to rebut victim character evidence. White said that such a concern was too speculative and hypothetical to be taken seriously by the Court. Since nothing like that happened in the lower courts during this case, White believed Powell's concern to be completely unconnected to the facts of the *Booth* case.

Justice Antonin Scalia joined in White's dissent, but he also wrote his own dissenting opinion in which he insisted that the amount of harm an offender causes is precisely related to his or her personal responsibility. Scalia gave the example of two bank robbers who try to kill a guard. The first one aims his gun and pulls the trigger, but the gun jams and the bullet never leaves the chamber. The second robber also aims and pulls the trigger, but in this instance the gun fires and kills the guard. Both shooters intend to and attempt to do the same thing, and morally they are equally blameworthy. However, one will be charged with attempted murder and the other with murder, which carries a much harsher punishment. The first robber will not be as harshly punished because his actions did not cause the same degree of harm. Scalia pointed out that many factors in death penalty cases are not directly related (or even related at all) to moral guilt. For example, many laws hold accomplices in crimes responsible for capital offenses their partners commit. This, Scalia maintained, is not unfair because it is related to how much harm the offender caused, and hence it is related to his or her blameworthiness.

Scalia ended his dissenting opinion by describing the victims' rights movement as a democratic manifestation of what the American people want. He castigated the Court for trying to silence the voices of victims by suppressing their testimony and trying to conduct "the debate on the appropriateness of the capital penalty with one side muted."

Two years after *Booth* was decided, the Supreme

Court revisited this issue in the case of *South Carolina v. Gathers* (490 U.S. 805, 109 S.Ct. 2207). Demetrius Gathers had been convicted of murdering a self-styled street minister named Richard Haynes. Gathers and three companions came upon the mentally troubled Haynes in a park and viciously beat and sexually assaulted him. Later, Gathers returned and stabbed Haynes to death. At the time, Haynes was carrying some religious plastic statues, two Bibles, rosary beads, and some religious tracts.

At the trial the religious articles were admitted into evidence without any fanfare, simply as objects scattered near the body and as circumstantial proof that after the beating the offenders had rummaged through Haynes's belongings looking for something of value to steal. It was not until the sentencing phase of the trial that the prosecutor called specific attention to the articles. He spoke at length about the victim's religious commitment and read, word for word, the printed text of a prayer the victim carried with him. He also pointed out that Haynes was registered to vote, trying to lead the jury to the conclusion that Haynes had been a good citizen. Later, Gathers's lawyers argued that the state's references were improper.

The question for the Supreme Court in *South Carolina v. Gathers* was whether the defendant could fairly be punished more severely because of the prayer or the voter's registration card the victim was carrying. In other words, would it have been a less serious crime if Gathers had done the same things to a person who did not happen to have a prayer in his pocket or a voter's registration card in his wallet?

Following *Booth*, Justice William Brennan, writing for the majority, found the state's use of these objects impermissible because it shed no light on the circumstances of the crime and had nothing to do with Demetrius Gathers's personal responsibility or moral guilt. Even though in this case it was the prosecutor himself (rather than friends or family) who made statements concerning the victim's personal characteristics, the Supreme Court decided that the statements violated the Eighth Amendment because they "could result in imposing the death sentence because of factors about which the defendant was unaware, and that were irrelevant to the decision to kill." Part of Brennan's reasoning was that Demetrius Gathers had no idea what was in Haynes's pockets when he assaulted and murdered him. Brennan observed that it had been dark in the park, and even as Gathers went through Haynes's belongings and scattered them across the bike path he probably still did not know what was printed on the pieces of paper. For these reasons Brennan determined that, like the evidence in *Booth*, the objects carried by Richard Haynes were "wholly unrelated to the blameworthiness" of Demetrius Gathers and were therefore not properly considered at his sentencing hearing.

There were two dissenting opinions in *Gathers*. Justice Sandra Day O'Connor believed the majority had gone too far when it said that the Eighth Amendment disallowed *any* discussion of the victim. She interpreted *Booth* as forbidding extensive discussion by and about the victim and his or her family. But that did not mean, she reasoned, that any reference to the individual character of the victim was irrelevant or that the victim had to be reduced to a "faceless stranger" in order to comply with the Eighth Amendment. O'Connor did not think the prosecuting attorney's remarks were the kinds of statements the Supreme Court disallowed in *Booth*. Antonin Scalia also wrote a strong dissent, insisting that *Booth* had been wrongly decided and that it was not simply constitutional, but actually extremely appropriate, for a court to consider the specific harm done and the admirable personal characteristics of a particular victim when determining a fair punishment for the offender.

SHELBY COUNT
DATE
08 29
IUSI COMPLE
96421196 01
B OKING UP
MEMPHIS TENNES

RETHINKING VICTIM IMPACT STATEMENTS: PAYNE V. TENNESSEE

Pervis Payne spent June 27, 1987, waiting in the Memphis, Tennessee, apartment of his girlfriend and watching the apartment across the hall. When Charisse Christopher and her two small children came home, Payne entered the Christophers' apartment and made sexual advances toward Charisse. She resisted, and he attacked her and the children with a butcher knife. Charisse and her daughter were killed, but her son survived in spite of the brutal wounds inflicted on him. Pervis Payne was convicted of two counts of first-degree murder for the deaths of Charisse Christopher and her two-year-old daughter, Lacie, and of assault with intent to murder Charisse's three-year-old son, Nicholas.

During the penalty phase of his trial Payne put on four witnesses: his mother, his father, his girlfriend, and a psychologist who had treated him while he was in prison. Payne's witnesses talked about what a good person Payne was and how he had never been in any kind

Mug shots of Pervis Payne, whose appeal of his murder conviction and death sentence led to a stunning reversal of Supreme Court rulings on the admissibility of victim impact evidence.

77

Chief Justice William Rehnquist, author of the Supreme Court's 1991 Payne v. Tennessee *decision. That decision allowed sentencing juries to hear evidence on the individuality of the victim and the impact of the crime on victims and their families.*

of trouble before. The psychologist talked about Payne's very low IQ and about what a polite person he seemed to be.

The state of Tennessee presented testimony from Charisse's mother. The prosecutor asked her how three-year-old Nicholas had been affected by the murders of his mother and sister. Charisse's mother testified that Nicholas cried for his mother and sister and that he did not seem to fully understand their deaths or that they would not be returning home. In his closing arguments, as he urged the jury to sentence Payne to death, the prosecutor emphasized the effect of the crimes on Nicholas. He reminded the jury that the child was conscious at the time of the murders and had seen and heard the entire attack. The state emphasized Nicholas's loss, asking the jury to focus on the "burden that that child will carry forever" (501 U.S. 808 at 816). The jury returned a death sentence.

Payne's attorneys appealed his conviction and sentence, arguing that the admission of the grandmother's testimony and the state's closing argument constituted prejudicial violations of his Eighth Amendment rights as interpreted in *Booth* and *Gathers*.

In June 1991, the Supreme Court handed down its ruling in the case of *Payne v. Tennessee* (501 U.S. 808, 111 S.Ct. 2597). Although just two years had passed since its *Gathers* decision, the Court overruled that and the *Booth* decision, deciding that victim impact statements were, indeed, constitutional.

Chief Justice William Rehnquist wrote the majority opinion in *Payne v. Tennessee*. Rehnquist began his argument by discussing the relationship between "blameworthiness" and the degree of harm caused. He recalled the dissenters' argument in *Booth*, which claimed that it is fair and appropriate to take into account, when determining the appropriate punishment, how much harm a person actually caused. Rehnquist repeated Scalia's example of a person aiming a gun and pulling the trigger with the intent to kill, but having the gun misfire. Although that shooter is just as "blameworthy" as another shooter who successfully kills his or her victim, Rehnquist observed, the unsuccessful shooter will not get the same punishment, because, significantly, less actual harm has been done.

Rehnquist asserted that the measure of harm is always relevant at two stages in criminal punishment. First (as in the misfiring-gun example), it is relevant when determining what crime the offender will be charged with, which defines the appropriate range of punishments. Second, it is relevant for the sentencer to know exactly how serious the offense is when determining how severe the specific punishment should be. Rehnquist also observed that the majority of states seemed to want victim impact information, having passed laws enabling sentencers to consider information about the harm caused by a defendant's crime.

Rehnquist further argued that the majority had misread legal precedent in *Booth*. Although the capital defendant's right to be treated as a "uniquely individual human being" was upheld in *Woodson v. North Carolina*, "it was never held or even suggested in any of our cases preceding Booth that the defendant, entitled as he was to individualized consideration, was to receive that consideration wholly apart from the crime which he had committed" (501 U.S. 808, 822). The *Woodson* decision, Rehnquist declared, was about how much information to include in consideration, not about excluding information. In other words, *Woodson* addressed the unlimited amount of mitigating evidence a defendant could present—it allowed Pervis Payne to enter any testimony he believed would help the jury see him as a unique person, such as the testimony of his parents, his girlfriend, and the psychologist—but it was never meant to limit the aggravating evidence the state could present.

Rehnquist dismissed the concern that victim impact evidence would encourage juries to place differing values on victims' lives, depending on how worthy they thought the victims were. In the *Gathers* case, for example, the jury had sentenced the defendant to death even though the victim, Richard Haynes, was "an out of work, mentally handicapped individual, perhaps not, in the eyes of most, a significant contributor to society, but nonetheless a murdered human being" (501 U.S. 808 at 823-824).

States determine criminal sanctions, Rehnquist argued, and state legislators are free to include victim impact evidence as "simply another form or method of informing the sentencing authority about the specific

harm caused by the crime in question" (501 U.S. 808, 825). Quoting O'Connor's dissent in Gathers, Rehnquist declared that the victim should not be turned into "a faceless stranger at the penalty phase of a capital trial." He also quoted the Tennessee Supreme Court (which had upheld Payne's conviction and sentence), saying, "[I]t is an affront to the civilized members of the human race to say that at sentencing in a capital case, a parade of witnesses may praise the background, character and good deeds of Defendant (as was done in this case), without limitation as to relevancy, but nothing may be said that bears upon the character of, or the harm imposed, upon the victims" (791 S.W.2d at 19). However, Rehnquist did limit the *Payne* decision by saying that it applies to the first two kinds of evidence discussed in *Booth* (evidence on the individuality of the victim and evidence on the impact of the crime on

The Booth *and* Gathers *decisions, Justice Antonin Scalia (above) declared, had severely conflicted with the public's sense of justice.*

"[H]arm to some group of survivors is a consequence of a successful homicidal act so foreseeable as to be virtually inevitable," wrote Justice David Souter (at right) in rejecting the argument that a defendant should not be punished for facts about the victim of which he or she was unaware.

the victims and their families) but does not address the third kind of evidence disallowed by *Booth* (the victims' and their families' opinions about the criminal and the appropriate punishment).

Justice Sandra Day O'Connor joined Rehnquist's majority in the *Payne* decision, but she also wrote a concurrence to explain that she had a slightly different point of view. O'Connor did not think that all victim impact evidence should always be allowed, but she agreed with the majority that the Eighth Amendment does not automatically forbid any such evidence.

Like Rehnquist, O'Connor declared that states should be allowed to decide what kinds of evidence to present to the sentencing authority, though a small percentage of victim impact evidence could be improper (if it is so prejudicial that it will make the sentence fundamentally unfair). If a particular defendant thinks the evidence was unfairly prejudicial, he or she can appeal the sentence as a violation of due process under the Fourteenth Amendment, rather than as cruel and unusual punishment under the Eighth Amendment. In Pervis Payne's case, O'Connor concluded that the evidence presented at the sentencing hearing was not overwhelmingly prejudicial or unfair.

Justice Antonin Scalia wrote a two-part concurrence. In the first part he insisted that it had been unfair for the Court to refuse to allow relevant aggravating evidence during capital sentencing while at the same time allowing all mitigating evidence. Even if the Court addressed that injustice by limiting the admission of relevant mitigating evidence, however, he would still affirm the lower court's judgment because of his broad and fundamental belief that the Eighth Amendment allows the people of a state to decide what is a crime and what makes some crimes worse than others.

In the second part of his concurrence, Scalia defended the majority's abrupt reversal of Booth and Gathers. Among other arguments, Scalia pointed out that the earlier decisions had severely "conflicted with a public sense of justice keen enough that it has found voice in a nationwide 'victims' rights' movement" (501 U.S. 808 at 834).

Justice David Souter rejected the idea that facts unknown to an offender should not be used as a measure of blameworthiness. In his concurrence, Souter argued that while a criminal may not know the specific details about a victim's family, he or she certainly knows that "[m]urder has foreseeable consequences" (501 U.S. at 838).

> The fact that the defendant may not know the details of
> a victim's life and characteristics, or the exact identities
> and needs of those who may survive, should not in any

Angrily dissenting from the Court's Payne *decision, Justice Thurgood Marshall declared that victim impact statements can improperly focus the jury's attention on "such illicit considerations as the eloquence with which family members express their grief and the status of the victim in the community."*

way obscure the further facts that death is always to a 'unique' individual, and harm to some group of survivors is a consequence of a successful homicidal act so foreseeable as to be virtually inevitable. (501 U.S. at 808)

Souter emphasized that only two of *Booth*'s three categories of evidence had been found admissible. While evidence about the unique characteristics of the victim and the impact of the crime on the victims' survivors is relevant to the offender's blameworthiness, the third category (how the survivors felt about the crime or the appropriate punishment) is not relevant, and it should never be allowed.

Souter argued that the *Booth* holding was unworkable. Usually, since a sentencing authority is the same jury that sat during the guilt phase of a trial, a great deal of evidence about the victim and the impact of the death would already have been presented. For example, in *Gathers* the information about the prayer and other religious items in the victim's pocket had already been given to the jury, since it had been presented as physical evidence strewn about the crime scene. Souter declared that "*Booth* promises more than it can deliver" by saying that the courts will exclude any facts about the victim unknown to the defendant. In order to truly honor *Booth*, all sorts of normal contextual details (details necessary for a fact finder to make sense of a crime) would have to be kept from the jury. If the rule of *Booth* requires that any information not available to the defendant at the time of the crime be suppressed from the jury, Souter argued, it would certainly lead to extremely arbitrary decisions.

In a very angry dissent, Justice Thurgood Marshall defended the holdings in *Booth* and *Gathers*. Marshall vehemently argued that the point of *Booth* and *Gathers* had been the important principle that "the sentence of death must reflect an individualized determination of the defendant's personal responsibility and moral guilt and must be based upon factors that channel the jury's discretion so as to minimize the risk of wholly arbitrary and capricious action" (501 U.S. at 845 [internal quotation marks omitted]). Marshall reasoned that, relevant or not,

> the probative value of such evidence is always outweighed by its prejudicial effect because of its inherent capacity to draw the jury's attention away from the character of the defendant and the circumstances of the crime to such illicit considerations as the eloquence with which family members express their grief and the status of the victim in the community.

In other words, as Justice Powell had explained in

his original decision in *Booth*, the problem with this kind of evidence is not that it is irrelevant or unimportant, but that it is so upsetting to the jury that it raises the risk that their sentencing decision will be unfairly tilted against the defendant. Marshall voiced his frustration with the *Payne* majority's primary argument—that punishment is often based on an assessment of the harm caused by the defendant. He asserted that neither *Booth* nor *Gathers* conflicted with that observation. Rather, they excluded one fairly narrow category of information (evidence about the victim's personal characteristics) in the course of capital punishment decisions.

Finally, Justice Marshall repeated his argument that while victim impact evidence may be important for many reasons, the risk that it would exert illegitimate pressure on the jury and lead them to focus on improper considerations such as the victim's standing in the community outweighs all other considerations. When a jury is deciding whether a defendant should live or die, argued Marshall, the entire inquiry should center on the defendant, not the victim.

Justice John Paul Stevens also dissented, writing a powerful opinion that attacked the majority for its decision. Stevens argued that it was improper for the Court to so casually overturn the previous two decisions, but even apart from the *Booth* and *Gathers* decisions, the *Payne* majority's decision, he declared, "represent[s] a sharp break with past decisions" (501 U.S. 808, 856). Stevens was incredulous at the majority's willingness to allow prosecutors to "introduce evidence that sheds no light on the defendant's guilt or moral culpability, and thus serves no purpose other than to encourage jurors to decide in favor of death rather than life on the basis of their emotions rather than their reason." Reversing the logic of the majority, Stevens created an interesting hypothetical example. Suppose, he argued, that a cold-blooded murderer attempted to offer evidence about the

Victim impact evidence, Justice John Paul Stevens declared in his Payne *dissent, is irrelevant to a defendant's guilt, inappropriately introduces emotion into the sentencing decision, and increases the risk that the death penalty will be applied arbitrarily.*

immorality of his victim. In this scenario, the murderer does not claim it was his victim's immorality that made him commit the murder (he did not even know about it at the time of the killing), but he has since found out bad things about the victim. Anyone could see, Stevens argued, that such evidence would be irrelevant and should be inadmissible. The same reasons, he claims, make the kind of victim impact evidence relied on by the prosecutors in *Payne* irrelevant and inadmissible.

Stevens argued that throughout the history of this country, courts have struggled to ensure that capital punishment be inflicted only when it is based on reason, rather than caprice or emotion. The long-held belief in the United States is that the only evidence properly considered at a death penalty hearing is evidence related to the character of the offense or the character of the offender.

Stevens conceded that the argument relied upon by the majority has "strong political appeal"; nevertheless, it should have "no proper place in a reasoned judicial opinion" (501 U.S. 808, 859). He disposed of Justice Scalia's arguments about the unfairness of letting in an unlimited amount of evidence about the defendant but very little about the victim by pointing out, "The victim is not on trial; her character, whether good or bad, cannot therefore constitute either an aggravating or a mitigating circumstance" (501 U.S. 808 at 859). In a harsh indictment of Scalia's logic, Stevens declared that his colleague wanted to measure the strength of the criminal justice system by looking at how many death penalties it generates. "Because the word 'arbitrary' is not to be found in the constitutional text, he apparently can find no reason to object to the arbitrary imposition of capital punishment" (501 U.S. 808 at 859).

Stevens was deeply troubled by the majority opinion's assumption that the courts must strive to provide an even balance between the prosecution and the defense in a criminal trial. The Constitution provides so many safeguards for criminal defendants because individuals are considerably weaker than the powerful state that prosecutes them. A criminal defendant is up against the police, the district attorney's office, and all of the resources available to the state. That is why the state is required to prove its case beyond a reasonable doubt and why there are so many other rules protecting people who have been accused of crimes. Stevens felt that the majority had misunderstood the criminal trial system if they thought they were supposed to provide a level playing field for the two sides' competition.

The two problems with victim impact evidence, Stevens maintained, are its irrelevance (because much of it will be unknown to the defendant at the time of the crime) and its unavoidable arbitrariness. He feared that such evidence "cannot possibly be applied consistently in different cases" (501 U.S. 808, 861). He reiterated the difference between capital sentencing and all other kinds of punishment, emphasizing that any decision making must be especially directed and limited in order to prevent the death penalty from being applied unfairly.

According to Stevens, the majority's examples—a person shooting a gun with the intent to kill but having it misfire, and a person driving recklessly and by sheer luck not killing anybody—aren't relevant to this case. (The majority claimed those examples showed that considering the harm done to a victim was traditional when assessing blameworthiness.) First of all, the majority's examples involve foreseeability. The reckless driver and the gunman both *know* that what they are doing could cause grave harm. This makes them different from the defendant who does not know anything about the specific circumstances of a particular victim. And second, in the examples, the decision to punish one act more severely than another was made by the elected, representative legislature and published as law so everyone had proper notification that the rules were stricter and the punishments harsher for people who succeeded in carrying out their illegal acts. The facts that potential criminals were on notice and that the decision was made by the legislature distinguish the stricter punishments from punishments based on victim impact evidence. Finally, in those cases every defendant who is convicted for actually performing the prohibited act will be punished in the same way. Similarly, every defendant who unsuccessfully attempts to break the law will also be punished in the same way as every other "attempted" felon. This distinguishes these scenarios from identical defendants charged with identical crimes where there is victim impact evidence. The problem

with this evidence is that only some victims will participate, and some will be more convincing than others.
The fact that victim impact evidence relies so heavily
on emotion makes it less trustworthy as a just and fair
indicator of guilt; it introduces an unpredictable and
potentially destructively emotional element into the
punishing decision.

Justice Stevens also disagreed with Justice Souter's
concurrence on two main points. First, he observed
that if every *defendant* knows that his or her victim's life
is unique and beloved, then so does every *juror*. Second,
he disputed Souter's claim that *Booth* is unworkable
because suppressing all information about the victim in
a criminal trial is often impossible. Stevens reminded
Souter that as long as details about the victim are relevant to the offense, they have always been and will
continue to be allowed into evidence. For example, the
horror of the crime in *Payne* meant that the mere
recounting of the facts gave the judge and jury a fair
dose of the obvious impact on the surviving victim.
Given that fact, it was unnecessary to dwell on how
awful the crime was in special testimony during the
sentencing phase. Victim impact evidence might not
have made a difference in the *Payne* case—the jury
might have voted for a death sentence even without
the grandmother's testimony about the impact on
three-year-old Nicholas—but Stevens insisted that the
Supreme Court's decision must be concerned with cases
in which such evidence *would* make a difference. In
those cases, Stevens argued, some defendants will arbitrarily, and therefore unfairly, be sentenced to die on
the sole basis of an emotionally effective victim impact
statement—evidence that should have been inadmissible because it was irrelevant to the defendant's guilt.

Stevens ended his argument with a strong chastise-
ment of the majority, which, he said, had gotten swept
up in popular anticrime hysteria. Public support for
capital punishment may be prevalent, but it is the leg-

islature's job to respond to public opinion, while the Supreme Court should be concerned only with the truthful interpretation of the Constitution, Stevens insisted. Because he believed the Court had made its decision on considerations other than constitutional meaning, he concluded his opinion by lamenting, "Today is a sad day for a great institution."

7.

ALTERNATIVES

Convinced that O. J. Simpson had murdered his son Ron—despite Simpson's acquittal in criminal court—Fred Goldman (shown here with his wife Patti at Ron's grave) filed and won a wrongful-death lawsuit against the former football star. In general, however, civil litigation isn't a practical option for victims dissatisfied with the outcome of a criminal case against the accused perpetrator.

In the United States today, the field of victims' rights continues to evolve, spurred largely by the demands of grassroots organizations. Victims are a powerful and sympathetic constituency, and politicians are generally eager to appear supportive of their goals. The victims' rights movement also dovetails with the anticrime agendas of many politicians, particularly conservatives.

In the eyes of many, victims' rights advocates are locked in a struggle with their perceived adversaries: defendants and their rights. The ground between these two distinct groups is seen as contested and tightly limited. Conventional wisdom says that when one group makes advances, the other necessarily loses ground— that any right gained by victims is a right lost by defendants, and vice versa. This is a common way to solve problems in America's "adversarial" legal system, but it is not the only way—and it may not be the best way— to regulate interactions between victims and offenders.

93

Nor do all victims believe that pursuing their victims' rights in the criminal justice system is best for them personally or best for society as a whole. When her small daughter was killed by a drunk driver, Candy Lightner realized that the problem of drinking and driving didn't get enough attention, and she decided to do something about it. She founded MADD (Mothers Against Drunk Driving), a group composed of mothers who have lost children in alcohol-related traffic accidents. Though MADD may be seen as an organization of surviving victims, its goals and accomplishments go beyond victims' rights. MADD focuses on *preventing* drunk driving. While it has campaigned to increase penalties for drunk driving, it also spends millions of dollars on educating people about the dangers of drinking and driving through commercials, billboards, posters, and other forms of popular social education. MADD has also inspired several offshoots, including SADD (Students Against Drunk Driving), which focuses on alerting young people to the dangers of drinking and driving.

Sometimes, becoming involved in the victims' rights movement politicizes people and stimulates them to become active in causes not directly related to their personal experience. Ellen Levin's 18-year-old daughter Jennifer was killed in New York's Central Park by Robert Chambers in a widely publicized case that became known as the Preppie Murder. As part of his defense, Chambers claimed that Jennifer Levin had willingly gone with him to the park and that he had accidentally killed her during "rough" but consensual sex. Because the victim's consent is a defense to the charge of rape, women who press charges for sexual assault are frequently subjected to painful questions from defense attorneys. While most states have enacted "rape shield" laws, which disallow any questions about a rape victim's past sexual conduct, women still complain that the criminal justice system puts them,

Shoes of all shapes and sizes line the rotunda of Florida's capitol in mute witness to the hundreds of victims claimed by drunk drivers in the state during 1995. The display was organized by Mothers Against Drunk Driving, a group founded by Candy Lightner after her daughter was killed in an alcohol-related traffic accident.

rather than their attackers, on trial. And in the Preppie Murder case, the victim was deceased and the crime was not sexual assault, so the rape shield laws did not apply. Chambers was exercising his right to construct a defense to the charges, but in the meantime, Ellen Levin laments, "the memory of my beautiful daughter was being dragged through the mud, and my family and I were helpless to do anything about it." Levin worked to help pass a New York state law preventing deceased victims and victims of nonsexual crimes from having their sexual histories brought out in court, and she also worked for the admission of victim impact statements

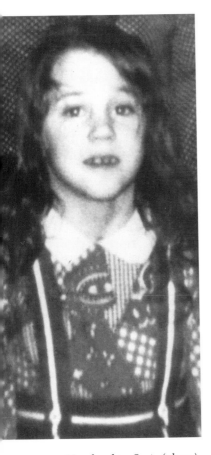

Her daughter Susie (above) deserved a better memorial than a state-orchestrated death, Marietta Jaeger (facing page) said in explaining her opposition to the execution of the person who kidnapped and murdered her little girl.

at sentencing. Both of these measures can be seen as being directly related to her experiences with the courts. But Levin also helped establish a political action committee called Justice for All, which campaigns not simply for fair treatment of crime victims, but for "tough on crime" measures as well. For example, the group worked to pass in New York a version of "Megan's Law," which requires that convicted sex offenders register with their local police departments after they get out of prison and that communities be notified of their release.

Another murder victim's family member who became involved in more generalized political work is Roberta Roper, who founded the Stephanie Roper Committee for Victims' Rights after her 21-year-old daughter was raped and murdered. The committee advocates traditional victims' rights, but it is also an extremely conservative group that, over the years, has worked to tighten parole rules, provide tougher sentences for various crimes, and make it easier for prosecutors to put convicted murderers on death row. Roper also lobbied (unsuccessfully) to change Maryland law so that it would require only 9 jurors to agree to a death penalty (instead of a unanimous 12). More recently, Roper's group has lobbied for more money for the state's victim-compensation fund, for a provision allowing appeals of judges' decisions about victims' rights, and for an anti-stalking statute.

A victims' organization that takes a completely different approach, Murder Victims' Families for Reconciliation, was established by Marie Deans after an escaped convict killed her mother-in-law, Penny, in South Carolina. The group believes that there is an alternative to violent revenge, and that alternative is better for everyone individually and for the community as a whole. Speaking of the person who murdered her mother-in-law, Marie Deans points out that he had a family too. "If he was executed, it would be another

murder. It would be worse in a way, because he would be put on death row and the family would have been told every day for ten years—or eight years or six years or however long it takes—that he was going to be killed. I think that's worse."

Proponents of reconciliation feel that the best long-term solution to the pain and suffering experienced by survivors is not state execution. Marietta Jaeger, whose daughter Susie was kidnapped and murdered, said that she did not want the executioner to write her little girl's legacy, that her child deserved a better memorial than a state-orchestrated death. Dorothea Moorefield, whose 19-year-old son was shot and killed in a restaurant in 1967, explained, "I have looked at the death penalty from every viewpoint. In the years since my son's death I have felt hatred, I have felt rage, and I have felt an overwhelming desire for vengeance. These are normal emotions for a victim's family and friends. But they are emotions that must be worked through and left behind if healing is to take place." Discussing the execution of a man who had killed a mother of four from the four children's point of view, Moorefield observed, "We owe those children more than a lesson in violence. . . . We need to be sure that they have what they need both physically and mentally to grow into adulthood without being destroyed by the crime that killed their mother."

Another alternative to pursuing victims' rights in the criminal justice system is civil litigation. In a criminal trial, the state prosecutes a person accused of breaking one of the state's laws and, if that person is found guilty, punishes him or her. The victim is little more than a witness to the crime that was actually committed against the state. A civil trial is fundamentally different. One person (the plaintiff) thinks he or she has been wronged by another (the defendant) and takes this private dispute to the state, which essentially acts as a referee. A civil trial can be between Mr. Jones and his neighbor over who owns a particular tree growing between their houses, or between Mr. Jones and Mrs. Jones over who is the best person to have custody of their children. It can also involve harm caused by a criminal act.

One of the problems with a civil trial is that it can only yield monetary damages—no one ever goes to jail as the result of civil litigation. Rather, one person is ordered to make the other person "whole" by paying him or her money in compensation for the harm done.

Another problem is that winning a judgment in civil court doesn't necessarily mean that the plaintiff will ever collect the money. No judge's order can transform a poor defendant into a person of means. In many, if not most, cases, this makes civil litigation impractical as a way for victims unsatisfied with the outcome of the criminal case to pursue the offender. Many people who commit crimes simply do not have a lot of money to pay their victims.

Of course, there are exceptions. O. J. Simpson, the former football great, actor, and TV personality, was acquitted of the charges of murdering his ex-wife, Nicole Brown Simpson, and her friend Ronald Goldman. But the victims' family members were convinced that Simpson had committed the crimes, and he seemed to have quite a bit of money, so they decided to pursue civil damages against him.

There is a danger associated with this kind of civil trial. Many victims talk about wanting finality and closure, and initiating a civil suit is hardly the way to ensure that a victim can return to his or her normal way of life. When the jury in the O. J. Simpson criminal case returned a not guilty verdict, Fred Goldman, Ron Goldman's father, had called it the second-worst day of his life (the worst being the day his son was killed). By initiating a civil suit against Simpson, Goldman set himself up for the possibility of having the third-worst day of his life—if the civil jury returned a not liable verdict. In the end, however, the jury in the civil trial found Simpson liable for the deaths of Nicole Brown Simpson and Ron Goldman, and he was ordered to pay the plaintiffs $33.5 million in damages.

Regardless of the verdict, though, civil trials are potentially quite painful for plaintiffs who were criminally victimized. Because the size of damage awards is related to the harm the defendant has done, smart civil lawyers who want to show the jury how much their client has suffered will deliberately prompt him or her to revisit the trauma in great detail. During a criminal trial, a rape victim might be troubled at the matter-of-fact way in which the crime is treated. If she later pursues civil damages, she may not appreciate the microscopic attention her own lawyer will want to pay to the fear and humiliation she experienced.

Another possibility for some crime victims is to initiate a "third-party" suit. In this kind of civil litigation, a crime victim sues someone other than the actual criminal offender. For example, in November 1974 a famous singer, Connie Francis, was raped at knifepoint in a hotel room in Westbury, New York. The rapist was never caught. Francis believed that the hotel was partly responsible for her attack because of inadequate security; the rapist had been able to enter her room through a window. She sued Howard Johnson's, a large hotel chain that operated the hotel where she was attacked, eventually settling her case for $1.5 million. Although this

Recovery

In a long-term study reported in 1994, psychologists Fran H. Norris and Krzysztof Kaniasty measured crime victims' symptoms at 6-month intervals, starting 3 months after the crime, then again 9 months after the crime and 15 months after the crime. They found that recovery tended to level off after nine months. If a victim is still having sleeplessness and anxiety attacks nine months after being victimized, chances are that he or she will continue to have those symptoms. The study found that rape victims' anger, embarrassment, depression, guilt, and fear were still present three years later.

Because of the enormous psychological strain violent victimization creates, victims are more likely than the general population to engage in self-destructive or anesthetizing behavior. They have higher rates of substance abuse, suicide attempts, and eating disorders.

Studies have repeatedly shown that good mental health care is essential for a full recovery from the trauma of victimization. It appears that the normal social resources people use to relieve stress are ineffective for crime victims. Often friends and family members are reluctant to talk about the subject; sometimes the victim may be embarrassed to bring it up. In any case, crime victims' psychological difficulties are often hard for a layperson to understand. Yet most crime victims do not receive any professional counseling. One survey suggested that only 12 percent of crime victims had contact with mental health professionals. Other studies, including a 1990 study by Fran H. Norris, Krzysztof was no substitute for seeing her attacker punished by the criminal justice system, Francis probably hoped that her civil litigation would impel Howard Johnson's—and other hotel owners who heard about her award—to increase security measures. This in turn would reduce the number of similar attacks in the future.

However, this approach can be seen as rather cynical because it assumes that the hotel owners would never bother to increase security unless they got sued. Also, some people think the plaintiffs in third-party suits are simply greedy. On the other hand, it might be argued that everyone who stays in hotels is safer as the result of Francis's lawsuit, because hotel owners realized that it was less expensive for them to increase security (and patron safety) than to pay large damages in lawsuits.

Another response to the growing clamor for victims' rights has been the development of a new kind of

Kaniasty, and Deborah Scheer, have suggested that just 2 to 7 percent of all crime victims, or 9 to 18 percent of severe crime victims, get in touch with counselors. The people most likely to seek help were victims of violent crimes who were depressed.

Violence takes something away from its victims that can never be restored. But that doesn't mean that victims must forever be worse off than before. Some victims report that with great effort and the help of others they have been able to transform their horrible experience into an opportunity for growth, increased self-knowledge, and understanding and compassion for others.

In his foreword to *Invisible Wounds: Crime Victims Speak,* Dr. Martin Symonds writes, "I have found there are undisclosed, open wounds of victimization kept open by the victim's self-hatred, guilt, and shame. These open wounds retard and prevent the healing process from taking place." However, in her introduction to the same volume, Susan Salasin, a victim of crime herself, offers a more optimistic version of recovery—if the victim can learn to talk about his or her experiences. Salasin describes how a victim's rage, helplessness, guilt, and fear can "ferment and materialize into new personality strengths." Victims may never regain the sense of invulnerability or false security they had before they were attacked, but those qualities can be replaced with positive traits.

semiprivate resolution process called victim-offender mediation. These programs allow criminal defendants to avoid or reduce public prosecution or punishment if they agree to participate. A growing number of jurisdictions offer victims and offenders the opportunity to meet, outside of court proceedings, and attempt to achieve some resolution on their own. Typically, they are asked to agree on an appropriate restitution, and sometimes nothing else is asked of either the victim or the offender.

There can be more to these interactions, however. By accident or by design, the meetings can be extremely emotional for the victim, the offender, or both. Ideally, the offender is able to see his or her restitution as something other than a court-imposed fine. Possibly, the victim gets an opportunity to see the offender in a more humane context, which could help resolve some of the emotional upheaval the crime has caused.

Victim-offender mediation certainly allows victims a more central role than does a state-run trial. Victims might find participation in mediation much more emotionally satisfying than testifying at a criminal hearing. However, there is a cost for these benefits, and these programs are sometimes criticized as easy solutions to problems that are actually quite difficult. Law professor Jennifer Gerarda Brown argues that mediation puts pressure on victims to "forgive" offenders, makes it difficult for them to have the satisfaction of a state condemnation of their violators, and degrades and diminishes state power by putting it at the service of private individuals. It may be harshest, however, for offenders. By agreeing to participate, offenders temporarily leave the court system. They may leave behind (or at least think they are reducing) the chance of receiving state punishment, but they also leave behind the procedural safeguards and protections the state offers people who have been accused of crimes. For example, offenders are not allowed lawyers, and they

At stake in the struggle over victims' rights is the extent to which victims' private grief and anger should play a role in the public process of criminal justice.

may be pressured to make "confessions" that could later be used against them in court. Worst of all, argues Brown, is the uncertainty that governs these proceedings. Neither offenders nor victims are clear about how much of a victim-offender mediation will get back to the judge in the court system, and both may be afraid of appearing uncooperative, unreasonable, or unwilling to make amends. Brown suggests that the best way to correct the problems with victim-offender mediation is to make these mediations absolutely voluntary and to keep them completely separate from the criminal proceedings.

Some versions of victim-offender mediation do avoid the problems described above. In parts of Australia, for example, certain juvenile offenders are offered the opportunity to participate in what are called Family Group Conferences. These conferences are attended by the juvenile offender, the victim, each of their families (or a support group, such as friends and counselors), and a police officer. The conferences are available only to offenders whose crimes are not too serious. The goal of the conference is to activate the normal social controls that are supposed to make people behave decently. The conferences attempt to be fairly neutral and nonjudgmental toward the offender. The hope is that, if given an opportunity to confront what he or she did in the presence of his or her own family and the family of the victim, the offender's own natural tendency will be to feel ashamed.

The shame felt by the offender is not meant to be a humiliating punishment. Rather, the system relies on the notion of "reintegrative shaming," a concept put forward by sociologist John Braithwaite, which assumes that most people genuinely respond to social disapproval and their own consciences. Obviously there has been a breakdown in the normal social controls, and authorities in Australia hope that Family Group Conferences will help young offenders learn, or relearn, those useful emotions, which can be powerful tools for changing behavior.

Whether or not alternative resolutions such as victim-offender mediation become more widespread, such resolutions will never be the legal outcome in more than a small fraction of the estimated nine million violent criminal victimizations each year in the United States (and they will be reserved only for the least serious of these offenses). Similarly, victims who channel the pain of their experiences into community or political action will probably always constitute a minority.

Inevitably a much-larger proportion of crime victims—especially those who have suffered violent victimizations—will want to exercise their rights within the criminal justice arena. Many, no doubt, will see this as their best chance for recovery, but the criminal justice system wasn't designed to support the emotional needs of victims. The adversarial nature of American trials requires that only evidence deemed relevant be admissible, that witnesses speak only in response to questions asked of them, and that the defendant's lawyer be allowed to interrupt in order to voice objections, making it unlikely that a victim will be able to satisfactorily talk through his or her trauma in court. And, despite the recent changes affording victims a greater role in the process—changes that in some cases have received the approval of the U.S. Supreme Court—many victims and victims' rights advocates remain dissatisfied with the level of participation they are currently permitted; they seek even greater rights. At the same time, defense lawyers and some constitutional scholars express dissatisfaction with what they see as inappropriate victim participation in the criminal justice process, and they fear that further concessions to victims can only lead to a trampling of the rights of the accused.

The struggle between the two groups is unlikely to disappear anytime soon. Ultimately the issues will have to be resolved in the courts or in the halls of Congress. At stake is the very character of American criminal justice: will it remain primarily a public process, or will the private needs and wishes of victims be given a more central role?

Bibliography

Baldinger, Beth, and D. Thomas Nelson. "Victims and Violence: Crime Victims and Psychological Injuries." *Trial* 31 (February 1995): 56.

Brown, Jennifer Gerarda. "The Use of Mediation to Resolve Criminal Cases: A Procedural Critique." *Emory Law Journal* 43 (1994): 1247.

Erez, Edna. "Victim Participation in Sentencing: Rhetoric and Reality." *Journal of Criminal Justice* 18 (1990): 19.

Ford, David A. "Prosecution as a Victim Power Resource: A Note on Empowering Women in Violent Conjugal Relationships." *Law & Society Review* 25 (1991): 313.

Freedy, John R., et al. "The Psychological Adjustment of Recent Crime Victims in the Criminal Justice System." *Journal of Interpersonal Violence* 9 (1994): 450.

Henderson, Lynne N. "The Wrongs of Victims' Rights." *Stanford Law Review* 37 (1985): 937.

Moore, David B. "Shame, Forgiveness, and Juvenile Justice." *Criminal Justice Ethics* 12 (1993): 3.

Neiderbach, Shelley. *Invisible Wounds: Crime Victims Speak.* New York: Hawthorne Press, 1986.

Norris, Fran H., Krzysztof Kaniasty, and Deborah Scheer. "Use of Mental Health Services Among Victims of Crime: Frequency, Correlates, and Subsequent Recovery." *Journal of Consulting and Clinical Psychology* 58 (1990): 538.

Silver, Roxane L., Cheryl Boon, and Mary H. Stones. "Searching for Meaning in Misfortune: Making Sense of Incest." *Journal of Social Issues* 39, 2 (1983): 81.

Table of Cases

Arizona v. Superior Court of the State of Arizona, The Honorable William L. Topf, and Jafet Adolfo Coronado Court of Appeals of Arizona, Division One, Department D (1996 Ariz. App. LEXIS 178; 223 Ariz. Adv. Rep. 25).

Booth v. Maryland 482 U.S. 496 (1987).

Gardner v. Florida 430 U.S. 349 (1977).

Payne v. Tennessee 501 U.S. 808 (1991).

South Carolina v. Gathers 490 U.S. 805 (1989).

Woodson v. North Carolina 428 U.S. 280 (1976).

Index

Index

Index

Picture Credits

SARA FAHERTY teaches legal research and writing to first-year law students at the State University of New York at Buffalo and is working toward a Ph.D. in American Studies. She holds a B.A. in English Literature from Wellesley College and a law degree from SUNY-Buffalo's Law School. Faherty also spent several years practicing law, focusing on complex litigation.

AUSTIN SARAT is William Nelson Cromwell Professor of Jurisprudence and Political Science at Amherst College, where he also chairs the Department of Law, Jurisprudence and Social Thought. Professor Sarat is the author or editor of 23 books and numerous scholarly articles. Among his books are *Law's Violence, Sitting in Judgment: Sentencing the White Collar Criminal*, and *Justice and Injustice in Law and Legal Theory*. He has received many academic awards and held several prestigious fellowships. He is President of the Law & Society Association and Chair of the Working Group on Law, Culture and the Humanities. In addition, he is a nationally recognized teacher and educator whose teaching has been featured in the *New York Times*, on the *Today* show, and on National Public Radio's *Fresh Air*.